Old Ways, New Days

Old Ways, New Days

A Family History of Gypsy Life in South London and Kent

Rosie Smith & Lindsey Marsh

Cover photo: The Smith family, Yaldon, Kent, 1940s

First published by Francis Boutle Publishers
272 Alexandra Park Road
London N22 7BG
Tel/Fax: (020) 8889 7744
Email: info@francisboutle.co.uk
www.francisboutle.co.uk

Old Ways, New Days: A Family History of Gypsy Life in South London and Kent
© Rosie Smith and Lindsey Marsh, 2009

All rights reserved. No part of this book may be reproduced, stored
in a retrieval system, or transmitted, in any form
or by any means, electronic, mechanical
photocopying or otherwise without the prior permission of the publishers.

ISBN 978 1 903427 45 3

The authors

Rosie Smith and Lindsey Marsh are second cousins. Their grandmothers, Minty and Emily Smith, were sisters, born into the travelling way of life, from a long line of Romany Gypsies. Rosie lives on a gypsy site in Surrey, along with her family and parents Levy and Lily Smith (Ripley). Although Lindsey was not brought up as a Gypsy she is proud of her heritage and is researching her Gypsy roots. She lives with her family in a house in Telford, Shropshire.

This book is dedicated to

Levy and Lily Smith a mum and dad to be proud of – Rosie

Gran Emily Smith and all her chavvys! – Lindsey

And all our Gypsy family who we both are very proud of – Rosie and Lindsey

Contents

  3   List of illustrations
  6   Preface
  8   Romany Rokker
11   Introduction
13   Our Family Story
18   The Traditional Gypsy Lifestyle
30   Gypsy Musicians
43   Bare-knuckle fighting
47   Hopping Down in Kent
56   Deaths and Funerals
59   In the Spotlight
72   Gypsies and discrimination
85   Poems
88   Picture Gallery
95   Further Sources
97   Acknowledgements

List of illustrations

6 The Smith family and their wagon
11 The Ripley family in dartford Woods
12 A modern trailer
13 The marriage certificate of Darby (Derby) Smith and Eliza Cooper
14 The marriage certifiate of Alfred (Elf) Smith and Charlotte Lee
15 1891 Census showing Alfred and Charlotte Smith
15 Elf (Alfred) Smith
16 1901 Census showing Alfred and Charlotte Smith
17 Charlotte Smith with her son Henry, 1920s
18 Bill (Mousey) Smith and family outside his wagon
19 Crown Derby
19 Smith family inside their trailer, Star Lane site, 1970s
20 Aaron Smith in trotting cart
20 Jasper Smith with family and pony
21 Joe Ripley, dog breeder, 1950s
21 Tom 'Tommer' Gregory with pups, 1950s
21 Joe Ripley
22 Levy Smith and son Levy with truck, 1980s
22 Levy Smith with 'Sharpers Joe's' sons, Joe's Johnny, and Alf at Star Lane site, Kent, 1970s
23 'Fox's Wally', Louise Smith, Lena Cooper, Mary Smith and children, Fill Common, Surrey
23 Mosey Smith with grinding barrow
25 Bill Reynolds with wife Caroline (Carline) and friends round a 'yog'
26 Sarey-Ann Cooper (grandmother of musician Ambrose Cooper) with 'tikna'
27 Rhymer Stockins with his daughter, Maryann
27 Pearly Smith in strawberry field, Kent, 1970s
28 Minty Smith in old age
28 Minty Smith with her youngest daughters Lou and Bobos

28 The Smith sisters: Amy, Rachel, Emily
29 Members of the Smith and Ripley families, 1940s
30 Nelson Smith making pegs, watched by Aaron 'Bonza' Smith, 1940s
31 Aaron Smith making holly wreaths
32 Pegmaking: Nelson Smith with Nelson Duval as a child
33 Jasper Smith making pegs with his cousin Henry Smith
33 Betsy Smith and son cooking on a 'yog'
34 Young Ambrose Smith with his brother Mushy, granny Sarah-Anne and aunts Amy and Esther. Morden 1950s.
36 Joe Smith playing the accordion
37 Folk singers, Minty and Jasper Smith
38 The Smith family carrying on the musical tradition
38 A new generation. Sherrymarie Smith, a rising star
39 Sherrymarie Smith at a gypsy fair
39 Cover of a CD by Sherrymarie Smith
40 Derby Smith with his father Jasper
43 Bare knuckle champion Bartley Gorman
44 Mark Ripley after one of his fights
45 Mark Ripley with his son, Mark 'Tarzie', 1980s
46 Henry Smith with his wife in the Kentish hop gardens, 1940s
47 George Ripley in the hop fields, 1950s
48 Nelson 'Mushy' Smith outside a hop hut, 1950s
48 Hop picking on a Kent farm. Members of the Cooper-Smith family
49 Hop pickers Bill Reynolds and his wife Caroline (Carline)
49 Rosie Smith 'hopping' in Kent
50 Lily (Ripley) Smith sitting on a hop bin, 1950s
50 Levy Smith stopping in a cherry orchard, 1991
51 Gypsies in a cherry orchard, Pembury, Kent
52 Bill Reynolds cherry picking, Pembury, Kent
53 Rosie Smith, aged 15, in a cherry orchard, Pembury, Kent, 1989
53 Levy Smith with his wife Lily and cousin Rosie
54 Levy Smith with his cousin Buddy and brother-in-law Joe Ripley in a cherry orchard, Pembury, Kent 1980s
56 Photograph taken at the funeral of one of the Stockins (Smith) family
57 Unrania Boswell (on crutches) at the funeral of her husband, Levi
58 Funeral of Levi Boswell, St Giles' church, Farnborough
59 Emily Smith (daughter of Derby and Eliza)
60 Emily Smith with grandson Tony
61 A real character, Emily Smith on one of her birthdays
62 Rose Ripley with her grandchildren Rosie and Sam
63 Sam and Rose Ripley, 1960s
64 Levy Smith aged 12
64 Levy Smith
65 Brothers, Levy, Aaron and Jasper Smith with friends

66 Lily and Levy Smith with a wagon made by Levy
67 Levy Smith acting the clown
67 Levy Smith
68 Levy Smith with five of his brothers, two sisters, his mum and aunt Emily and her two chavvys
69 Jasper Smith
70 Jasper Smith – a man of great status in the Romany community
72 Jasper Smith with his son, Jasper, Epsom, Surrey
73 Rosie Smith aged three with her mum Lily, 1970s
74 Levy Smith shaving in the chrome of his trailer, 1970s
76 Norman Dodds MP talking to Rose Ripley and her son George, Dartford Woods
77 Norman Dodds MP with the Ripley family
7   Funeral of Norman Dodds
78 Rose Ripley with councillors before eviction from Dartford Woods
78 The eviction
79 The eviction from Dartford Woods
79 Gypsies stopping along the A2 after they had been evicted from Dartford Woods
80 Jasper Smith, a Gypsy soldier in the Second World War
83 Levy and Pearly Smith
83 Stopping in a cherry orchard, Pembury, Kent
84 Aaron Smith in a toy 'silky'
88 Lindsey Marsh with Dan and children Shannon and Danny
89 Rosie Smith aged 18 with Rosie Baker
90 Pearly (Rosie Smith's daughter) inside their chalet
91 Levy Smith (Rosie Smith's brother)
92 Stopping in Kent
92 Jasper Smith withn his son and grandchildren
93 Gypsy children, Star Lane site, Kent, 1970s
94 Rachel Smith and family, Kent, 1962
98 'Fair Play' Smith, Bill Smith, Alf Smith, Alice Smith and Louie Smith, Surrey, 1930s

Preface

Whenever I read a book, 'over-thinker' that I am, I always get to wondering about the person who wrote it. Well I thought just in case there was someone like me that reads this book, I would tell you a little about me and why I have written this book with my cousin Lindsey.

I was born a Gypsy, married a Gypsy, and I'm living a Gypsy lifestyle on a site in Surrey. I got married to my husband Aaron in the travelling way when I was seventeen, and like most Gypsy girls I was pure on me wedding night. Me and Aaron have three beautiful *chavvys*, our oldest is Pearly and she is sixteen and getting married to a lovely Gypsy boy, Sonny James, next year and I have my little goldfinch Sherrymarie who is eleven, then my baby is my *mush* who is named Aaron after his dad and he is six.

In my life I have a lot of things that mean a lot to me like; my best mate Betsy Smith and her family; and music and singing and dancing, I guess, because I have grown up with it around me, because all my family are music lovers. I also love poems and writing too, but I'm not sure where I got the love for that from. Maybe it's from listening to my dad's stories all of my life, and maybe I like poems because they are like songs in a way. I'm not sure, I just know I have always loved reading and writing them. Although all of the things I have just said are important to me, the most important thing to me before and above anything else is my family and I love each and every one of them to bits and I am proud to call them my family, just like I am proud to call myself a Smith and am proud of the Ripley in me too. I am proud of all the Gypsy people in my history that without them I would not be here today and I am proud to say I have some wonderful people in my family, people who deserve to be remembered and written about, and that is one of my many reasons for writing this book with my cousin Lindsey who I didn't know existed until a few short months ago but who I feel I will always have a bond with

The Smith family and their wagon

now because of this book. It's a funny story how Lindsey and I met and this book came about. It all started with me putting a video of some of my many family photos on YouTube and a message being left from a girl saying she was glad to see the people in the photos on YouTube as they were her family. So I write a message back asking who she was and the answer that came back was that she was my great aunt Emily's granddaughter who I had never seen before. After I write back to Lindsey telling her who I was, we got chatting on the internet of all places and she asked me if I had ever thought about making a book out of all my Gypsy family photos as she was sure there were people out there that would love to see them. When I got off MSN to her, I thought about what she had said and I know I would love to write a book, not only about the photos but about a dying way of life, a true story of how Gypsies really were. I knew there were many books about Gypsies but everyone I have ever read had been written by *gorgers* and how can someone who has never lived our life tell it how it really is. For days I thought about what Lindsey had said to me about the book and although I wanted to do it, I kept asking myself 'how could a *needie* girl, who had never been to school much, just a month now and then, write a book?' But my heart kept answering me, with the help from a cousin who has been to uni page by page. So I went on the net and sent my cousin Lindsey a message asking if I was to write the book, how would she feel about writing it with me, I waited for (what seemed like days but was just a few hours) for her answer 'I would love to write a book about our family and Gypsy lifestyle with you' so that is how our book began.
Rosie Smith

I've been researching our family tree for sometime now and it saddens me that special people in our family (such as my own granny Emily) have been undervalued just because of their race. My good cousin Rosie for example is a very smart woman, and she's a better poet than most people I know (despite receiving very little schooling), yet her talents are often overlooked because many wrongly assume all Gypsies have low intelligence. My great uncle Jasper was also a very bright man, who probably achieved more than most people during his lifetime, yet he has often been viewed as a second class citizen, purely because of his race.

Rosie and I have therefore created this book, as we feel our family, and Gypsies in general, deserve more credit than what they are given. We have used our family (as just one example of a traditional Gypsy family) to outline the sort of life Gypsies have lived and what they have still managed to achieve, despite the persecution and difficulties in life they encountered.

I will always be grateful to Rosie for inviting me to write this book with her, not only does it finally give our family and Gypsies the recognition they deserve but it also combines my passion for my family and my dream to publish a book. This book also allows me to show my children and future children (currently just Shannon and Danny) and my baby sisters Jade and Abbie our Gypsy heritage and the wonderful people we have in our family today. Thanks Rosie for inviting me to write this book with you. x
Lindsey Marsh

Romani Rokker

Common Gypsy words and expressions with their English meanings.

Alaged	Ashamed	Dabbes	Fingerprints
Ark	Shut up/listen	Dal	Give
Atch	Stay	Daled	Hit
Atching tan	Stopping place	Davvs	Day
Avree	Away	Dikking	Looking
Bang	Devil	Diklo	Scarf
Besh	Sit	Ding	Throw
Bitti	Little	Dinlo/dinla	Stupid/fool
Bori	Big or pregnant	Dordi Dordi	Common exclamation
Bosh	Fiddle		
Brogues	Trousers	Doosta	Plenty
Bullos	Police	Drag	Car
Bung	Curse	Fams	Hands
Busty	Work	Fokey	People
Cams	Money	Forny/faumy	Ring
Chant/charm	Sing	Gatter	Beer
Chavvy	Child/baby	Gatterd	Drunk
Chickly	Dirty	Gavvers	Police
Chockers	Shoes	Gilly	Man
Chop	Exchange/swap	Glazier	Window
Chore/choring	Steal/stealing	Goona	Dead
Churkla	Bird	Gorger	Non-Gypsy
Clammed	Starved	Grub	Food
Clamming	Starving	Grunter	Old person
Cosh	Stick/wood	Gry	Horse
Covers	Things	Hobben	Food
Crank	Fool	Hotchi	Hedgehog
Cur on	Come on	Hummal	Hair
Cushty	Good/fine	Jasin	Going

Jass	Run	Pakish	Hungry
Jefro/jethro	Coat	Parni	Water
Jell/jel aki	Get away	Pen	Speak
Jib	Language	Pester	Pay
Jiggur	Door	Pogger	To beat or break
Jin	To know	Poggered	Broken
Jovell	Women	Pooker	Tell
Jubs	Head lice	Pookering kosh	Signpost
Jubby	Lousy	Poove	Field
Juk	Dog	Poov a gry	Put a horse out in the field
Kenick	Non-Gypsy		
Kel	To play/to do	Posh	Half
Kell	Sell	Poshers	Money
Kenner	House	Poshrat	Half Gypsy
Kitchemer	Pub	Praster	Run
Kom	Like	Pug	Run
Kor	Fight	Pug up	Hide up
Ladgful	Embarrassing	Pugging	Ferreting
Lelled/Loured	Arrested	Putcha	Ask/enquirePutsy
Loring	Stealing	Putsy	Pocket
Lovner	Money	Rakli	Girl/women
Lumbruss	Sugar	Rat	Blood
Luvney	Bad (easy) Girl	Rawnie	Posh lady
Mandy	Me/I	Rokker	Talk
Mandy's	Mine/I'm/My	Rokker Romany/ Romani	Speak the Romany language
Mass	Meat		
Mored	Killed	Rom	Gypsy man
Moro	Bread	Romani rye	Posh Gypsy
Mort	Woman	Rukker	Tree
Moui	Mouth	Savving	Laughing
Mogdy	Dirty	Scran	Food
Muller	Devil	Sham	Pretend
Mullered	Dead	Shav	Run
Mullering	Dying	Sherro	Head
Mung/Munging	Beg/begging	Shiv	Knife
Munge	Cuddle	Shoshi	Rabbit
Mush	Fella/bloke	Slang	Licence
Mushkas	Police	Slumicky	Dirty
Nantee	Don't	Sooti	Sleep
Nark	Bad person	Tan	Place/home
Narked	Upset	Tatcho	True/real
Narkri	Nasty	Tikna	Baby
Nav	Name	Tobar	Road/path
Needies	Gypsies	Togram	Clothes pegs

Togs	Clothes
Totter	Gypsy man looking for work
Totting	Looking for iron or work
Trash	Fear
Trashed	Scared
Tuvs/tuving	Fags/smoking
Vardo	Wagon
Vart	Look
Wafady	No good
Wittle	Carve out with a knife
Vonga	Money
Woodus	Bed
Yocks	Eyes
Yog	Fire
Yoro	Eggs

Introduction

Gypsy life in Britain has changed radically over the past century, you only need to compare the life of Gypsies in the 1500s to the present day, to agree

Above: The Ripley family in Dartford Woods (Left to right) Lily Smith (Ripley), Lily Ripley (Smith), Rose Ripley, George Ripley, Rosie Ripley and Sam Ripley

with that. The use of the language has slowly diminished, the way of living has changed dramatically and the way society has treated them has changed too. Some changes have been for the better, but many have been for the worse and so in general many agree the attitudes towards Gypsies, could still be better today.

From the old ways of the bender tents and horse-drawn wagons, to the new days of modern Gypsy sites and council houses, Gypsies have been forced to adopt a way of life which feels unnatural to them. Given the circumstances, Gypsies still achieve great things but are never given the credit they fully deserve. In many Gypsy families there are self-taught musicians, talented song-writers, natural singers, good hard-workers, fantastic cooks, loving mothers and caring fathers.

Through rare old photographs and personal stories, this book provides a real 'inside' account of what life has been like for Gypsies over the past century, sharing rare biographical and personal memories of lovable Gypsies, some of whom have now long gone. It also explores some of the prejudices towards Gypsies today, how they have been treated in the past, yet what they have still achieved despite of this.

A modern trailer

Our family story

Above: The marriage certificate of Darby (Derby) Smith and Eliza Cooper

The majority of people mentioned in this book are related and come from the Smith, Ripley and Cooper families – popular Gypsy names – and the following information provides useful family tree information about some of them.

Rosie Smith and Lindsey Marsh are second cousins. Their grannys were sisters: Rosie's gran Minty (the oldest) was born in 1911 and Lindsey's gran Emily (the youngest) was born in 1927. Minty and Emily were the daughters of Derby and Eliza Smiths.

Derby and Eliza

Eliza Cooper was born and christened in Walton on the Hill in 1890. At the age of 21, she married Derby Smith, a 22-year-old hawker. At the time of marriage, the couple were residing at Hachhurst Downs, and married in the parish church in the small village of Shere in Surrey. Derby's younger sister May also married at the same church just one month after, in the February 1890, to Ambrose Eldon.

Derby and Eliza went on to have seven children: Minty, Amy, Levy, Jasper, Rachel, Reuben and Emily.

The following two biographies describe the ancestors of Derby and Eliza.

Elf Smith, his Lottie Lee and the birth of Derby Smith

Alfred was the son of James Smith and to his friends and family he was better known as Elf (or Alf). Elf was born around 1854.

By his mid-twenties Elf had fallen in love with Charlotte (known as Lottie) Lee, the daughter of a Gipsy hawker and in 1879 the lovers officially married in Christ Church, Battersea. Sadly Christ Church was later destroyed by bombing at the end of the second world war.

Shortly after their wedding Lottie gave birth to their first child Jasper and went on to have more sons, Harry and Nelson.

Elf and Lottie lived a traditional Gypsy life, although it was hard at times living in their tent and providing for their family. To make money Elf would make chairs and baskets and would often go out hawking these door to door, while Lottie would tell fortunes. Fortune telling became very popular for a Gypsy woman to earn a living in the

Below: The marriage certificate of Alfred (Elf) Smith and Charlotte Lee

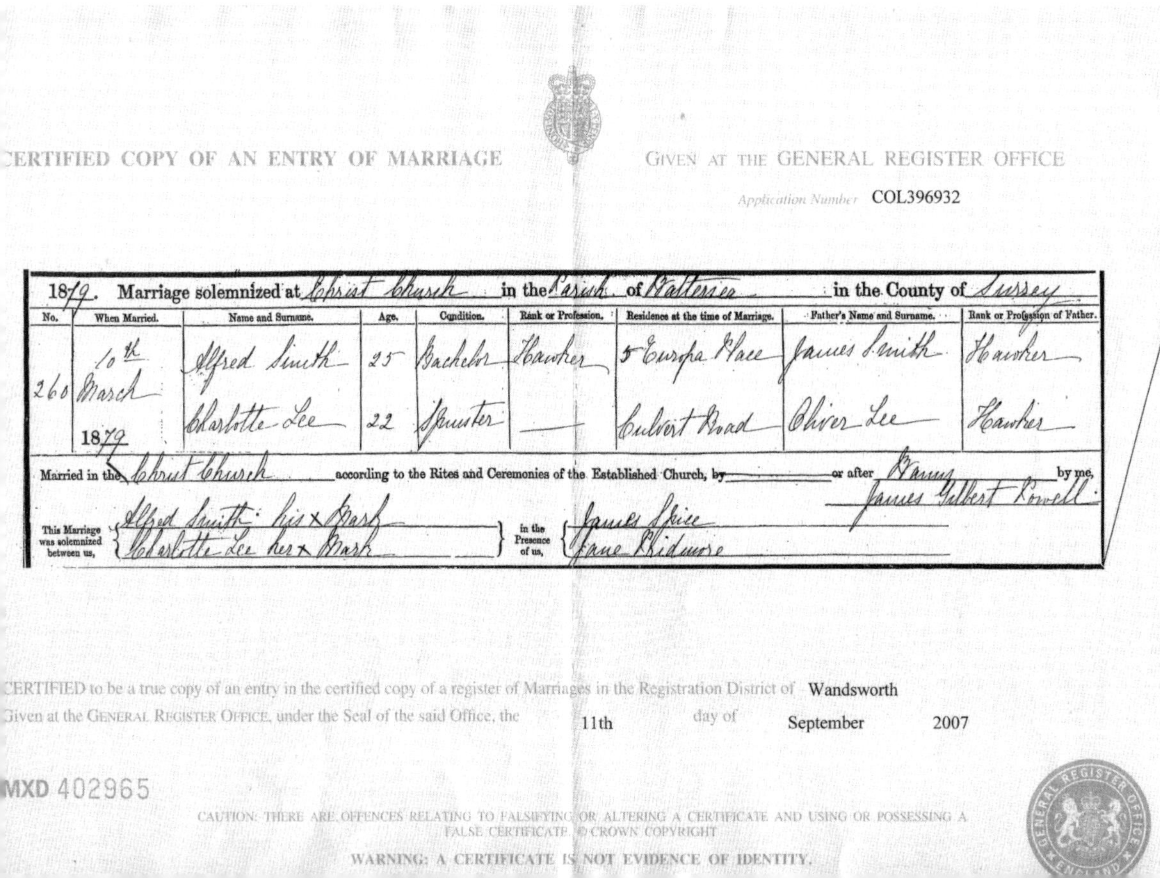
CERTIFIED COPY OF AN ENTRY OF MARRIAGE — GIVEN AT THE GENERAL REGISTER OFFICE

Application Number COL396932

1879. Marriage solemnized at Christ Church in the Parish of Battersea in the County of Surrey

No.	When Married.	Name and Surname.	Age.	Condition.	Rank or Profession.	Residence at the time of Marriage.	Father's Name and Surname.	Rank or Profession of Father.
260	10th March 1879	Alfred Smith	25	Bachelor	Hawker	5 Europa Place	James Smith	Hawker
		Charlotte Lee	22	Spinster	—	Culvert Road	Oliver Lee	Hawker

Married in the Christ Church according to the Rites and Ceremonies of the Established Church, by or after Banns by me, James Gilbert Powell

This Marriage was solemnized between us, Alfred Smith his x Mark, Charlotte Lee her x Mark — in the Presence of us, James Price, Jane Skidmore

CERTIFIED to be a true copy of an entry in the certified copy of a register of Marriages in the Registration District of Wandsworth

Given at the GENERAL REGISTER OFFICE, under the Seal of the said Office, the 11th day of September 2007

MXD 402965

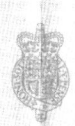

1880s as work on farms had started to decline.

On the road, Elf and Lottie travelled many places around London, including Fulham, Battersea and Surrey. In the summer, they would sometimes travel to the Epsom Downs which hosted the Derby horse race. The Derby took place the first weekend in June and Gypsies travelled there from all over southern England.

At the Derby, Elf would sell his wares and Lottie would tell fortunes. They'd make lots of money because thousands of people would attend. The horse racing was free to watch and there were Gypsy fiddlers, palmists and flower sellers.

Both Elf and Lottie always liked going to the Derby, not just for the money, but because they often met up with friends

Top: 1891 Census showing Alfred and Charlotte Smith. Alfred is described as a basket maker

Left: Elf (Alfred) Smith

1901 Census showing Alfred and Charlotte Smith

and family too. Epsom Downs had already been a popular stopping place for Gypsies for more than 300 years because it provided lots of open flat land which the travellers liked. Although Queen Victoria went to the Derby in 1840, it was only in Elf and Lottie's time that horse racing became popular on the Downs.

The year 1889 turned out to be a special year for Elf and Lottie, as Lottie gave birth to a beautiful baby who they named Derby. That year Tommy Loates won the race on Donavon, completing the 1 mile, 4 furlongs in 2 minutes, 44 seconds.

Amy Deakins & her Bundle Cooper. The birth of Eliza Cooper
Amy Deakins was a winter baby, born Friday 2 February 1866. At the time of birth Amy's parents, Thomas and Rachel (formerly Franklin), were stopping in Broad Green, West Croydon. Rachel was born in the mid-1840s. Her dad, Richard, was a wire-worker by trade, a job which a number of Gypsy men did during these times. Rachel's mum Lucy was born in Middlesex around 1826. In her childhood days Rachel travelled mainly between Surrey and Hampshire with her brothers Abraham, James and Job and her sisters Charlotte, Eliza and Lydia.

At nine months, Amy was christened in the local Christ Church in Croydon and by the time she was nineteen, she had four younger sisters: Rose, Rachel, Rebecca and Britannia and four younger brothers: Thomas, Abraham, Alfred and Leonard. Thomas being the eldest son, was named after his dad in true Romany tradition. Thomas and Rachel also named one of their daughters Rachel after her mum.

As a young girl Amy lived with her family in a Gypsy bender tent, which was only really used to sleep in at night. Amy quickly took on the role of mother to help raise her younger brothers and sisters and at night the family would gather around the warm fire

Charlotte Smith (Elf's daughter) with her son Henry, 1920s

to discuss the days events and to entertain each other. As a family they travelled around Croydon and then Mitcham in the 1880s. Amy's dad was a licensed hawker, and they stopped with lots of Gypsy families during his period, including the Parkers and Hoadleys.

As time went by, Amy married William (who was known to most as Bundle) and like most of the family, Amy and her husband started to settle around Mitcham. Amy's sister Rose married into the Powell family, her brother Abraham married into the James family and her sister Polly (Britannia) married Leonard Dixie, the son of Sarah-Ann Eastwood and Edward Dixie in 1903. Her sister Polly was born and baptized in 1883, and went on to live to the age of 102, surviving two world wars, witnessing five different kings and queens take to the throne and Britain change prime ministers more than twenty times!

In 1890 Amy and Bundle settled down to make a family of their own. Together they had a beautiful girl who they named Eliza.

Traditional Gypsy lifestyle

Right: Bill (Mousey) Smith and family outside his wagon

Below: Modern trailer. Travelling became easier in the 1950s when caravans replaced old horse-drawn wagons

By Rosie Smith

Gypsies hold a lot of things dear to them like their homes, china, animals, trucks and work, way of life, pride and respect, honour, weddings and dealings, but above all they hold dear their families.

Home

There is a saying that 'a man's home is his castle' and for Gypsies this is very true, for Gypsies take great pride in their homes, happily showing off a new trailer they have purchased to friends and family, everyone admiring it. Gypsies keep the inside of their trailers spotlessly clean and wash the outside down at least every two weeks, windows being washed almost every day in summer.

China

Gypsies love china and 'only the best will do', such as Ainslie, Minton, Crown Derby, and cut glass. Gypsy women take great care and pride in their china which they collect throughout most of their married lives.

Left: Crown Derby

Below: Smith family inside their trailer, Star Lane site, 1970s. (Left to right) Levy Smith, Joe Smith, Levy Smith senior, Noah Reynolds, Pearly Smith

It normally starts when first married and mothers pass down pieces to them, that their mothers gave to them, and family and friends also give china as wedding presents.

Animals

Gypsies have always had a great love for their animals not only because they are their pets, but because in the years passed, they have been a means to feeding their families and how would they of moved their homes without their beloved horses? Gypsy men are among the best horse men in the country knowing just how to break a horse in and are expert trainers.

Gypsy men train their trotting horses to a high standard for their Gypsy races. In the days passed, Gypsy men had their horses to pull their wagons and carts, picking strong cob horses to do this. But now wagons are no longer used, Gypsy men turn to trotting as a way of still using their much loved horse.

Gypsy men will get races on with other Gypsy men, for as little as a pint of beer or to as much as thousands of pounds. They will pick a long straight road to race on, most times the races will take place on a Sunday with other Gypsy men from other families coming to watch the race, all betting on who they think will be the winner. The cart

Top: Aaron Smith in trotting cart

Right: Jasper Smith with family and pony

used for the race is called a 'silky' which is a very light cart giving the horse plenty of room to pick up speed. Speeds such as 30 mph are reached. At the end of a race the men involved will shake hands and they will all probably end up in a pub because for Gypsy men the race is as much about loving the company of other Gypsy men as it is the race.

Gypsies have always kept animals such as birds, chickens, ferrets, and dogs. Their dogs and ferrets were used as working animals that often have helped feed the family; but now they are mostly used for sports such as ferreting, coursing and lamping, although the rabbits they catch are almost always eaten.

Me uncle Joe Ripley is a Gypsy dog breeder and trainer. All his dogs are trained to the highest standards.

Top: Joe Ripley, dog breeder, 1950s

Far left: Tom 'Tommer' Gregory, 1950s, with pups

Left: Joe Smith with Levy Smith (son of Lily and Levy)

Trucks and work

A Gypsy man's truck always plays a big part in his life, for most Gypsy men this is what they feed the ones they love with. My brother would always say 'long as I got me truck, mine will never go hungry' and I think this is how all Gypsy men see it.

Gypsy men from a young age are taken to work with their fathers and teach things such as scrapping, roofing, tree topping and tarmacing. Gypsy men have always been men that have many skills, always passing what they know on to their sons. This is why most Gypsy boys leave school at a young age, for their fathers feel by being at school they are missing out on learning what they will need to know to feed their families when men.

Gypsy men rarely work for a boss, as they find it very hard to take orders from another man and also because of the way they have been brought up free; they like to work their own hours, being able to take time off work whenever they choose.

Top: Levy Smith and son Levy with truck, 1980s

Right: Levy Smith with 'Sharpers Joe's' sons, Joe's Johnny, and Alf at Star Lane site, Kent, 1970s

TRADITIONAL GYPSY LIFESTYLE

Although Gypsy men always work hard, there are days they will wake in the morning and just decide that today they will take their children to the beach or they will go ferreting or such, whatever they felt like doing that day.

Lots of Gypsy men are as good under the bonnet of their trucks as a mechanic would be, although most have had no training in this; it is all self-taught or learnt from their fathers.

Way of Life

Although many things are changing for Gypsies, with many now living in *kenners* (houses) and on sites, still many try to hold on to a dying way of life, which is made so hard for them by new laws and government. For centuries, Gypsies have earned their living by knocking on doors selling, or offering their services such as sharpening knives and in later years fixing roofs, cutting down trees, laying drives,

Top: 'Fox's Wally', Louise Smith, Lena Cooper, Mary Smith and children, Fill Common, Surrey

Left: Mosey Smith with grinding barrow

but a new law passed in 2008 no longer allows this, so, many Gypsy men are now having to learn a new way of *calling* (looking for work).

Pride and respect
Pride and respect have always been very important things to Gypsies with children, who from a young age are taught to have respect for older people and family. They are taught to have pride in their self, their home, their families and about the fact that they are a Gypsy. Men and boys have great respect for Gypsy women and girls, with many rules on what is and isn't right to do; such as a Gypsy women would never stand and talk to a group of Gypsy men, no matter how well she knew them and Gypsy men on meeting the wife of a friend out, would only ever say a respectful 'hello' and never engage in a conversation. If a Gypsy man was to call on another Gypsy man and he was not home but his wife was, who was also a friend, the man out of respect for her husband would leave and come back when his friend was home, as it wouldn't be seen as proper for them to be seen alone together no matter how well they were friends. There are many more such rules all to do with pride and respect.

Honour
Honour is something Gypsies fight for. There is nothing most Gypsy men would not do to protect their honour, having high standards for themselves and their women. All Gypsy girls must be virgins on their wedding day and Gypsy men take great pride in the fact that they are the only man to have slept with his wife. They are proud of their daughters for keeping their honour and if a Gypsy girl don't, it brings shame to all the family, but more so to their fathers. Most Gypsy women keep their honour, not for their Gypsy men but because they also feel it's the right thing to do and have pride in their self because of it.

Weddings
Although it's becoming more the way with Gypsies to have big church or register office weddings, still you don't need to do either of these to be thought of as 'married' by other Gypsies. To us there is no 'living together as boyfriend and girlfriend', for as soon as you move in together, you are thought of as 'married'. Gypsies call it 'taking off'. A young boy and girl will decide they want to be married 'the Gypsy way', so will go off on the night and when they come back next morning everyone among the Gypsies will think of them as married. This can happen as young as fifteen, but the average age for a girl is seventeen and for a boy eighteen or nineteen. Girls as young as twenty-five will be thought of on the shelf. Although I have heard people say about 'jumping sticks' or 'jumping the broomstick', this is just a saying and what they really mean is that the girl and boy moved in together or went off like I just said and came back husband and wife … I'm not sure if Gypsies hundreds of years ago did 'jump sticks' or the 'broomstick' but if so, it has not been done in this country for years. One of the reasons I think why Gypsies see a girl and boy as married once they have spent the night together, is because it is our beliefs that a girl should only have sex with her husband and should be pure on her wedding night, so once a girl and boy have spent the night together they are

thought of as married. Divorce is very rare among Gypsies with most marriages lasting a lifetime.

Dealing
Dealing plays a big part in every Gypsy man's life, with many deals done just for the love of dealing. Always someone will have what is called 'the best of the deal'. Deals are done for lots of different things such as birds, dogs, chickens, horses, china, gold, trailers, cars, but most popular, trucks. Most times money will change hands, with the person who has the thing worth less money giving money to deal. Money is always given back for 'luck', meaning the person who was given the money, will give a small amount back to the man he has dealt with, to bring him luck with the deal, but this is only done when dealing with other Gypsies.

Many times have I heard my dad asked 'what have you got for sale Levy?' to which he would answer 'everything but the wife and *chavvys*! – this would be many old Gypsy men's answer, for they loved to deal and always hoping to have a good deal, by ending up better off than before they dealt, but even if they didn't this time, they knew they probably would next time!

Family
Family is the most important thing to all Gypsies, with children being the main focus in each family, and most Gypsy families all living close to each other. My mum and dad have four children; my oldest brother Levy Smith named after my dad (as are most old-

Bill Reynolds with wife Caroline (Carline) and friends round a 'yog'

Sarah-Ann (Sarey-Ann) Cooper (grandmother of musician Ambrose Cooper) with 'tikna'

est Gypsy sons), Joe Smith, Pearly Smith (Baker by marriage) and I am the youngest, Rosie Smith, and called the baby even at the age of 35. We all live on the same site with our parents, with even some of the married grandchildren living on the site, and many of the other married grandchildren living close by in houses. This is how most Gypsy families are, those in houses all buying or renting houses close to each other. Almost all Gypsy parents, knowing no sacrifice they would not make for their children, my mum and dad have always been there for me throughout my life and are now there for my children giving them all the love and support they need.

Respect to Gypsy women
When I think of all the women in my family, from a time and way of life long gone now, I can't help but feel great respect. It's true that life was hard for all Gypsies in the years passed, but it was the Gypsy women I feel that suffered the most. Gypsy girls would start cleaning and looking after younger brothers and sisters from a very young age, taking on the role of mother and cleaner until their own mother would return from hawking.

Although they worked hard as children, it was not until they became wives at ages as young as fifteen and sixteen that life really became hard for them. Almost every year a baby would be born until their bodies could no longer conceive children. They would give birth with little or no help, many dying in childbirth.

Pregnancy was not a reason not to work and most Gypsy women would go out hawking until they gave birth. Most times with a basket in their arms and baby tied to them in a blanket, they would walk for miles like this in all weathers *munging* whatever they could such as shoes and clothes and selling whatever their husbands had made for them to sell out of their baskets. They would have many doors slammed in their faces and insults spat at them but still go on to the next door with a smile forced on to their faces.

Many would tell fortunes making up whatever

Above: Rhymer Stockins with his daughter, Maryann

Left: Pearly Smith in strawberry field, Kent, 1970s

stories they thought the person wanted to hear and the better storyteller they were the more money they would earn.

At the end of their workday when they returned home, still their work would not be finished for they would still have the night's meal to prepare and children to wash for bed. Then at night, when they were so tired they would fall into bed, their husbands would want loving which for Gypsy women just meant the fear of another pregnancy.

They would wake next morning and cook breakfast on the fire their husbands had made for them, and then wash the children, then it would be another day of walking and tapping doors. In most Gypsy families, although the father was loved and was the head of the family it was the mothers that were adored by their children. My father has always spoke of his mother with great pride, love, and respect, and it is little wonder, for the old Gypsy women, truly were women to be admired.

Me granny Minty and sisters were said to be some of the most beautiful Gypsy

Above: Minty Smith in old age

Above right: Minty Smith with her youngest daughters Lou and Bobos.

Bottom: The Smith sisters (left to right) Amy, Rachel, Emily

women that were ever born. Me granny had three sisters Amy, Rachel and Emily, and except aunt Emily they were all as dark as night with coal black hair that was so long and thick that when let down, it hung down their backs like a blanket.

Me granny always was a beautiful women. When she died at the age of 89 you could still see the beauty in her. Aunt Amy even now at the age of 95 is a truly beautiful old woman.

All of the sisters lived hard lives, all having big families of children and struggling through the war, and after the war when times were hard, they were always worrying about where the next meal for the children would come from.

Granny, aunt Amy and aunt Rachel all went out with baskets over their arms, most times with a *tikna* in one arm and the basket in the other, tapping doors, selling pegs, wooden flowers or primrose baskets. Some days they would walk for miles trying to get enough money to take grub home for their *chavvys*, only to get back to where the wagons had been and find they had been moved on by the *gavvers*. Then they would have to follow the signs left for them by their families such as broken sticks pointing in the direction they had gone. All day they had walked and now they would have to walk again, until they found where the families had gone. Always their husbands would ask of the *gavvers* could they just wait until the women came back, but rarely would the *gavvers* agree to this.

Members of the Smith and Ripley families, 1940s. Both of Rosie Smith's grannies are in the photo. Minty Smith is looking out of the wagon

There are seven stages to making Gypsy pegs

1. First: Cut the wood from the copse, hazel or willow wood
2. Chop: Chop off the leaves and brush wood
3. Rind them: Strip off the soft bark or skin
4. Chop: Chop off to the peg length
5. Tie them: Put the tin bands around them, this is fixed with a small nail
6. Mouth them: Slit up to the tin to make the opening a "V" shape
7. Last: Now the last stage is the most difficult of all. That's the selling of them!

The Art of Peg Making

My father has told me when he was a boy, it was an everyday thing to see Gypsy men sat on the ground with wood shavings everywhere all around them, as they sat making pegs or wooden flowers for their wife or mother to take door to door in their baskets to sell.

Gypsies always used to live outside 'normal' society and learned to live with and from nature by poaching and taking just what we needed from the

Opposite page: Nelson Smith making pegs, watched by Aaron 'Bonza' Smith, 1940s

Top: Aaron Smith making holly wreaths

Pegmaking: Nelson Smith with Nelson Duval as a child

wild to survive, but no more. It was the same with our traditional crafts; whether peg making or flowers, we took from the hedgerows hazel and willow freely provided. This was working with nature. The more willow and hazel are cut the more it will grow.

Cooking

All old Gypsy women seem to be the best of cooks, maybe because they cooked so much for so many, all having big families in the days that have passed. Me mum always tells me what a good cook me granny Rose was, she says to me, me granny Rose could cook a meal good enough for a king to enjoy and I must say if her cooking was anything like me dear old aunt Kate's (who we lost a few years back) then she is right. I always remember how whenever I would go round me aunt Kate's, if she was cooking she would (without even asking me) get me a big dish or plateful out of whatever she was doing and I would look at it and think, I am never gonna get through it, she would pile the plate up so high, but still when I was finished there was never any left and truth be

Top: Jasper Smith making pegs with his cousin Henry Smith. As a boy Jasper would make money making pegs and wooden flowers

Left: Betsy Smith and son cooking on a 'yog'

told, I maybe could have found room for a little more it tasted that good!

Many times I have tried to cook a 'Joe Grey' or 'Bacon Pudding' like me aunt Kate used to; using all the same ingredients she did, but still somehow it never seems to taste as good as hers. I think the best tasting food used to be that what was done on the fire years ago, maybe because they was such good cooks back then and maybe because they only used all fresh homemade food, no supermarket food like today. Sometimes now in the summer, when we have a pull away in a field somewhere, me and me mum will get out our pots and do a bit of cooking on the old fire and I must say it always seems to taste better than when I cook at home on my electric cooker. I'm not really sure if it's the natural flames from the fire that makes it taste better or just because we enjoy the thought of it being cooked on the old *yog* like my old Granny would of done it years and years ago. All I know is we all seem to enjoy it and there is never any left!

Young Ambrose Smith (far right) with his brother Mushy, granny Sarah-Anne and aunts Amy and Esther. Morden, 1950s.

Recipe for Joe Grey
Joe Grey is a popular Gypsy recipe. It is a runny stew and is great with crusty bread and butter. Traditionally it is made with rabbit or chicken and also mushrooms, however it can be easily adapted to accommodate any left over ingredients you may have.

    Ingredients (for 4 people)
    6 rashers of bacon
    4 large tomatoes
    4 large sliced potatoes
    1 onion
    6 stock cubes
    8 mushrooms

Fry the bacon and onion in a pan until brown
Cover with water and add the potatoes
Simmer for 10 minutes
Add the tomatoes and mushrooms and sprinkle the stock cubes all over
Simmer gently for about 30 minutes, stirring occasionally
Add water if needed to keep the stew fairly runny.

Recipe for Bacon Pudding
Another popular Gypsy recipe.

    Ingredients (for 4 people)
    8 rashers of bacon
    2 big onions
    Suet
    Flour
    Pepper

Chop 2 onions into small pieces
Mix the suet and flour with a little water to make the pastry
Then roll out pastry
Lay bacon rashers across the pastry then lay the chopped onions across the bacon
Sprinkle pepper across the top
Wrap in cloth or kitchen foil
Put in pot in hot water and cook for 3 hours
Add water if needed.

Gypsy musicians

A love for music is born into Gypsies with most Gypsy families having at least one family member who can play an instrument, the accordion or guitar being the most popular. Not many Gypsies have training and most are self taught but still seem to play with skill, beautiful music.

Ambrose Cooper (Smith) *by Rosie Smith*

If someone was to ask me who was the best known Gypsy singer of all time, I would have to answer me cousin Ambrose, for there isn't many *needies* that ain't listened and enjoyed his songs. He is a Gypsy man that truly will go down in history for not only is he a singer, but a songwriter too, writing songs such as The Two Brewers and Old Motors. Now although I call him a songwriter, not one of his songs did he ever write anywhere but in his head, as Ambrose cannot read or write. But still this did not hold him back or stop him from becoming the truly greatest Gypsy singer of our time.

Growing up I never once thought about how well known as a Gypsy great he was becoming, to me he was always just my dad's cousin and good friend who would always drop in to me dad for a sing and dance. I have never known Ambrose to brag about his singing or songs and he has always just been happy to play for others as they sang. Me dad has spent many happy hours in his company, as have I.

Joe Smith playing the accordion, 1950s

Ambrose has never sang for money or fame, just for the love of it and can hardly ever be seen out without his guitar and is always ready for a song. Now his son Ambrose Jr is following in his father's footsteps and can't only play the guitar like his father but better.

I remember one night when I went to see Ambrose and his wife and their son young Ambrose was there and played for me along with his dad, and then on his own, never before have I seen a guitar handled with such skill or ease – it was like a part of him and I sat in bewilderment listening to his every note but the thing I found hardest to believe was that like his father, he has never had a lesson and they are both self taught.

Minty, Jasper, Levy and Darby Smith

Minty's brother Jasper was also known for his beautiful singing voice as was Minty and in the 1970s they made a record Here's Luck to a Man along with other *needies*.

Minty and her two brothers Levy and Jasper were all talented folk singers and were discovered over 40 years ago. They often recorded songs in Minty's home and because of their talent they were invited to sing on a number of albums. Jasper also appeared as a guest artist at a Loughborough Folk Festival.

Albums Minty, Levy and Jasper contributed to include:

Here's Luck to a Man. This was recorded by Mike Yates (Topic Records) in the 1960s and 70s. It included Minty, Levy and Jasper and other Gypsy singers including Joe and Lena Jones, Mary Ann Haynes, Chris Willett and Bill Ellson. Jasper's son Darby also sung on this album and played the guitar too.

Jasper's son Darby was also on the record singing his song he made up – Travellers in Heaven – a song still loved and played by

Top: Ambrose Cooper (Smith)

Left: Folk singers, Minty and Jasper Smith

Gypsies today, a song that will go down in Gypsy history, as will Jasper Smith who in later years got involved with fighting for Gypsy rights.

The Traveling Songster: An Anthology of Gypsy Singers. Released on LP in 1977 by Topic Records. Minty, Levy and Jasper sing on this album along with Phoebe Smith.

My Father's the King of the Gypsies (Voices of the People Vol. 11). This was reissued on CD in 1999. Tracks include: Minty, 'The Basket of Eggs'; Levy, 'The Haymakers', 'One Penny', 'The Game of Cards' and 'Georgie'; Jasper, 'Father had a Knife', 'Down in the Meadow', 'The Small Birds Whistle', 'The Squire and the Gypsy'.

The Rough Guide to Music of the Gypsies. This is a compilation of songs from different Romany singers from all around the world. Jasper and Levy not only sung on this

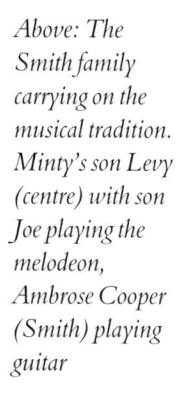

Above: The Smith family carrying on the musical tradition. Minty's son Levy (centre) with son Joe playing the melodeon, Ambrose Cooper (Smith) playing guitar

Right: A new generation. Sherrymarie Smith, a rising star

album, but used the mouth organ and played the drums too. Their tracks included 'Step it Away', 'Cock o' the North', 'Garryowen', 'Flowers of Edinburgh', 'Stop it Away' and 'The Girl I left Behind Me'.

To Catch a Fine Buck Was My Delight. Jasper sung 'Thornymoor Park'.

A Story I'm Just About to Tell. This album contains 24 different tracks and Jasper sung 'Hartlake Bridge'.

Sweet Gypsy Girl Singer Sherrymarie *by Rosie Smith*

Sherrymarie Smith is already an accomplished singer at the tender age of 10 years old. Her mature and expert voice has made her a hit with travellers and *gorgers* alike. She has attended many a Gypsy fair and festival and has gained rave reviews.

Now following in her great granny Minty's footsteps, Sherrymarie is singing her heart out. She is only ten years old but been singing since she could talk. Her voice is born talent and her granddad's second cousin Ambrose Cooper was the first to discover her, when at the age of four she asked him to play Coalminer's Daughter so she could sing to him. When she finished Ambrose was so impressed with her he made her sing it again and his very words were 'this baby got born talent'.

Sherrymarie made her first CD at the age of 8 and went around all the Gypsy horse shows across the country where she impressed lots of people with her voice and sold thousands of CDs. She sings all kinds of songs but country music is her first love like it is with most Gypsies.

Above: Sherrymarie Smith at a Gypsy fair

Left: Cover of a CD by Sherrymarie Smith

Old Motors
Ambrose Cooper (Smith)

Now you get some old motors a going everyday
But some of them you need a tow before you get away
I like a Bedford, don't mind an Aston
Long as she's a going, boys, she's good enough for me.

I jumped in my olf lorry drove it up to Horseman den outside of the gun
Up there I saw poor old Cowlow, he said he's had everyone
Little Nelson Barton had an old Beford van
He said I'll give you ten to chop, so boy I smacked his hand
I drove straight out of Horseman den jump straight across the green
I drove up into Galtist and this who I seen
I see old Franks Mosey outside of the pub
He had an old J2 boys she wasn't worth two bob
He said I just come up from Marden had a jpob to make it up the hill
I got a bit of money about me I'll have a chop and deal
I had a chop with Mosey gave him two quid back for luck

I drove straight out of Galtist in this old J2 truck
I drove back into Yalding flat out down Winstid hill
At the front of Yalding Bull I see Jakers Bill

Darby Smith playing the guitar with his father Jasper on melodeon

Inside there was old Levy, Jasper and his crew
All of old Jim Newlins boys and little snobby too
Old Stey was a playing his accorion stabnding against the door
Little Levy was dancing up and down the floor
Old Rhymea walked up to the bar with his cauliflower ear
The landlord said sorry jack there's no more beer served here
I like a Transit don't mind a Datson as long as she's going boys she's good enough for me.

Will there be any travellers in Heaven?
Darby Smith

Tonight as I stay by the roadside, just watching those travellers go by
Thinking what will become of those travellers, whenever their time comes to die
There's a master up yonder in heaven, got a place that we may call our home
But will we have to work for a living, or shall we continue to roam.

Will there be any travellers in heaven, any places which we may stay
Will there be any travellers in heaven, to move our old trailers away
Will the gorgers join with those travellers, will we always have money to spare
Will they have respect for those Gypsies, in the land that lays hidden uipthere?

Will there be any travellers in heaven, any pubs where we may get some beer
Or will there be the same old landlord, who says sorry no Gypsies served here
Will the travellers have to keep roaming, will we have to keep roaming around?
I'm so tired of roaming this country, I'd rather be under the ground.

Dikking at a needie
Rosie and Sherrymarie Smith

Well I like my loving done travelling style
and this little girl would walk a travelling mile
to find her a good old sweet talking travelling boy,
I said a travelling boy

I'm as bout as old fashioned as I can be
so I hope ya liking what ya see
cus when ya dikking at me
youre dikking at a needie

ya don't see no gorger when you dikk at me
cus a travellers what I am
I love running barefooted few the old Kent fields
and I love that travelling tan

well ya say I'm a made to fit your hands
but do a trailer on a site fit ya plans
cus if ya eyes are on me
ya dikking at a needie

Well this here site is a little full
but theres always room for one more
I'll show you a plot if ya show me a wedding ring,
I said a wedding ring

When it comes to love well I know about that
us travelling girls know where it's at ...
cus if ya dikking at me
youre dikking at a needie

you dont see no gorger when ya dikk at me
cus a travellers what I am
I love a running barefooted few the old Kent fields
and I love that travelling tan

well ya say I'm a made just to fit your hands
but do a trailer on a site fit ya plan
cus if ya dikking at me ya dikking at a needie
cus if ya dikking at me ya dikking at a needie

Bare-knuckle fighting

Gypsies have been involved in bare-knuckle fights for centuries, to the extent that many now class this as an 'ancient Gypsy tradition'. It has been widely written about in many books, from Pepys' diary to Jimmy Stockins book *On the Cobbles* in 2000 and Bartley Gorman's *King of the Gypsies*. Bartley was a Gypsy man that fought for honour and family pride, never for money. He was taught to fight at a young age and ended up being one of the best knuckle men in the country. He was a showman, inspired by Muhammad Ali to be more flamboyant and outrageous than anyone before him. Bartley dished out leaflets and challenged huge Gypsy gatherings from the back of a flatbed truck.

Most Gypsy men can fight from an early age and because of this it takes a very special man to become feared, even by Gypsies themselves. Mark Ripley is one of these special men who because of his considerable strength and bravery, is widely known and respected both in and outside of the Gypsy community today. Mark was born 11 May 1948 and given the fact he was so well known, yet died so young (at just thirty-four years old), he built up such a strong reputation in so little time.

Bare knuckle champion Bartley Gorman

Mark Ripley *by Rosie Smith*

My uncle Mark Ripley was known as a Gypsy man to be wary of by other Gypsies, for he was a man that if you got on his right side, there was nothing he wouldn't do for you, but if you upset him in any way, you knew you were going to pay and probably with a stay in hospital. He was known by Gypsies to be a brave man who seemed to have no fear of anything and would never back down from a fight or let another man get the best of him. If he was having a fist fight and the other man was getting the best of the fight, then he would turn dirty and bite or head butt or hit with anything he could get his hands on. Only the toughest Gypsy men would take him on and most that did were sorry they did afterwards.

I remember when I was about five or six and he was stopping in a field with about ten families of Irish travellers (something most English Gypsies wouldn't do on their own). When his hare coursing dog went missing he knew the dog couldn't get off its chain and that someone had taken it. He guessed right that one of the Irish travellers had taken it for they were well known for *choring* dogs at that time, so he walked over on his own to about twenty Irish men and told them that he was going to take his wife to shop and when he came back if the dog wasn't back on the chain there would be trouble. So my uncle Mark went to shop and when he came back in about an hour, the dog was back on the chain. Most Gypsy men wouldn't have dreamed of going to twenty men on their own like that, no matter if the men were English or Irish, for they knew they would be risking a good beating, but as I said, he didn't seem to have any fear, which he seemed to be liked and respected for by the Irish travellers.

Bartley Gorman talks of my uncle Mark in his *King of the Gypsies*. He names my uncle Mark as the best man in Kent and one of the most dangerous men in the country. He says of my uncle Mark 'He was the kind who would stand on his own against a hundred

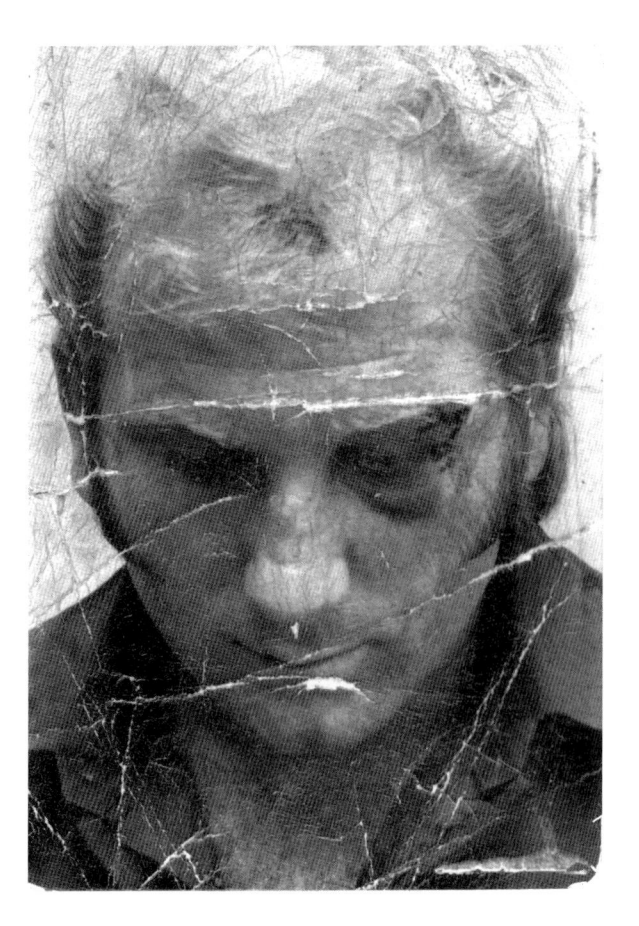

Mark Ripley after one of his fights

men rather than back down'. The Gypsy fighter Jimmy Stockins (who is my dad's second cousin), also talks of my uncle Mark in *On the Cobbles*.

My uncle Mark faced many dangerous men in his life but in the end he was killed by his own wife at the age of just thirty-four in 1983; but the memory of his bravery lives on and he is still talked about by Gypsies today and wrote about in many Gypsy books.

Mark Ripley's wife shot him dead in a pub in Croydon. It was not the first time she had attempted to kill him. The first time she shot him was a few years before when she had only wounded him and he had said to her 'if you ever shoot me again make sure and kill me cus if ya don't I'm gonna kill you!' On the night she killed him she walked in the pub with the gun and the people in the pub that saw her with the gun, got out of the way, but he just stood and faced her, laughed and said 'ya know what I told ya don't ya' and she did, so shot him dead to the pleasure of many that were scared of him, but to the great pain to those that liked and loved him.

Mark Ripley was my mum's baby brother and I feel proud to call him my uncle and I know not every day is a Gypsy man born like him.

Mark Ripley is a legend in his own right, who helped put Kent on the map and despite dying over twenty-five years ago, Mark is still idolised by many bare-knuckle fighters today.

Mark Ripley with his son, Mark 'Tarzie', 1980s

Hopping and cherry picking down in Kent

Hops were introduced to Kent in the sixteenth century and by 1724 there were 6,000 acres of hop fields in Kent alone.

Each summertime, many Gypsies and others would travel to Kent ready to pick the hops each August. Each hop-picking season would last for about four weeks and after being picked, the hops would be dried out in oast houses and used to help make beer.

Gypsies would often work in their large family groups, including the children and grandparents. The men would usually be employed as pole pullers, whose job it was to cut down the bines (which are large branches) ready for the women and children to pick the hops off to place in the large bins or baskets they were given. How much pickers would earn would then depend on how heavy these bins and baskets weighed.

Farmers would provide living quarters for all workers which varied from farm to farm, some providing barracks, tin huts, stables or barn and although some Gypsies would use the accommodation, most would use their own horse drawn wagons and bender tents.

Living quarters provided by the farmers were known as 'hop huts'.

Henry Smith, nephew of Darby and Eliza, with his wife in the Kentish hop gardens, 1940s

George Ripley in the hop fields, 1950s

By Rosie Smith

Me granny when young, like many other Gypsy women, worked out the hop fields with a *tikna* in one arm enrobed in a blanket, leaving the other arm free to work. All the family worked including the young *chavvys*, everyone doing there bit. They would do two fields a day to *gorgers* one. The farmers me granny and granddad worked for always

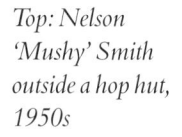

Top: Nelson 'Mushy' Smith outside a hop hut, 1950s

Right: Hop picking on a Kent farm. Young Ambrose Cooper is front, second left, with his mum, front first from right and other members of the Cooper-Smith family

Above: Hop pickers Bill Reynolds and his wife Caroline (Carline)

Left: Rosie Smith 'hopping' in Kent

Right: Lily (Ripley) Smith sitting on a hop bin, 1950s

Below: Levy Smith stopping in a cherry orchard, 1991

give them a good name, saying they was a tidy respectable family that worked hard.

The Smiths, Coopers and other Gypsy families worked in the hop gardens each year, as they were good hard workers who the farmers liked to have back and by the 1920s and 30s hop picking became most popular.

Although it was very hard work the families would still find time to enjoy life, the men going to the village pub on Sundays where horse dealing would go on outside, the men running up and down the road to show off the good points of their animals. Wads of *vonga* would change hands, the money always going to the head of the family. At the end of every hop picking me granddad would always leave Kent with a better horse, sometimes better wagon and always with money in his *putsy*.

After the second world war, however, tradition started to fade. By the 1960s machines had completely replaced the picking which had been traditionally done by hand.

Despite times when conditions were wet, muddy, cold and frosty, many Gypsies have very happy memories of those days.

Cherrying in Kent
Although the hop is the most common crop in Kent, Gypsies have also picked cherries, strawberries, apples and other fruit for decades.

Most summertimes, during the school holidays, Gypsy families would travel to the Kent orchards to go cherry-picking. This casual work provides a great way to earn cash in the hand whilst being outdoors. The work, however, can be physically demanding for those who want to earn lots, since workers get paid by 'piecework', which means the more you pick, the more you earn.

By Rosie Smith
Every summer for the first eighteen years of me life we did cherrying down in Kent and although the work was hard, I remember them summers as the best in my life.

When I was very young me father would work for the farmers, getting paid for each box of cherries our family picked, but as I got older he would buy the crop and work for himself, hiring pickers to pick for him, some of the pickers would be other Gypsy families and some would be hippies. At night when the work was done we would all sit round the *yog* an *rokker*, joke, or listen to the older ones tell stories and some nights me dad would play his accordion and we'd all have a sing song. On most of these times

Gypsies in a cherry orchard, Pembury, Kent

Bill Reynolds cherry picking, Pembury, Kent

Ambrose Cooper (Smith) would be there and play his guitar and sing his songs or just sing country songs. Me and my cousins would dance around the fire as he played, until I would get a smack round the ear from me mum and told to go dance away from the fire in case I was to trip an' fall in.

I've me best memories of the weekends, when on a Saturday night we'd go down to Yalding to the pub the Two Brewers, where we'd meet up with other Gypsy families such as the Reynolds, Bakers, Jones, Marines and many more that were down fruit picking, either cherries or strawberries.

Bill and his wife Carline (Caroline) worked on the farms in Kent for most of their lives, as did their children. They were one of the last families still working on the farms in the 1990s. They are a well respected Gypsy family that kept up Gypsy tradition for as long as possible.

The nights we spent in the Two Brewers were filled with more singing and dancing and just enjoying the company of people we liked, then on the Sunday if the weather

Top: Rosie Smith, aged 15, in a cherry orchard, Pembury, Kent, 1989

Left: Levy Smith with his wife Lily and cousin Rosie

was good, me father would take us to Yalding Lees (a Gypsy meeting place even today) where I'd paddle in the Lees with the other *needie chavvys* that were there most Sundays. Me father's first cousin on his father's side, Freddy Stockins, would be there with his wife and *chavvys* and I'd play with his gal Lisa, or every now and then on a Sunday, Kits, Lou would come down and bring her gal Kitty and I'd play with her.

It's all so long ago now but those times will always be in me head and heart.

I remember one summer when me dad had some hippies working for him. They was hard workers and me dad was pleased with 'em but when they got paid on a Friday they would stay drunk until the money was spent, which most times worked out to be Sunday night, but me dad didn't mind them drinking because they didn't cause any trouble and seemed always to be back to work on Monday. On one Wednesday though one of the hippies come to me dad and asks for a sub till pay day. Now my dad knew if he gave the man a sub he would get drunk and there would be no work done the next day, so me dad wasn't happy about giving him the money.

My dad asks the hippie why he wanted the money and the hippie said because they had run out of grub and hadn't eat since yesterday morning so me dad told him he wouldn't give them money but he'd sort them out with some grub so me dad and Buddy (Wally Smith), who my dad was in partners with in the cherries, took me dad's ferret and went rabbiting to make them a rabbit stew. They came back with four rabbits, made the fire up and put the pot on with water, put the rabbits in, then added potatoes,

Levy Smith with his cousin Buddy and brother-in-law Joe Ripley in a cherry orchard, Pembury, Kent, 1980s

carrots, mushrooms and onions. When the stew was done he told them all to bring their boils (bowls) which they did. Me father and buddy fed eight hippies that day an the next with the rabbit stew, until Friday came an they got paid. The hippie that asks me dad for the sub told me dad it was the best grub he had ever ate.

I've only been cherrying three times since I got married when I was seventeen, I think the last time was eleven year ago but there aint a summer in June that I don't long to go again and many times I will say that I am gonna go this year but what with me gal working and the other *chavvys* at school it never seems to happen. But still Buddy (Wally Smith) me dad's cousin and old partner goes every year, not for the money he earns for there's *nank* in cherrying now and he can earn more in many other ways, he just do's it for the love of it 'cus I think most who have done cherrying for a lot of years, like, we did always keep the love for it.

Deaths and funerals

By Rosie Smith

Gypsy men in the days long gone by were brought up to be strong and not to show weakness, so even at the funeral of a loved one you would rarely see them cry.

Old Gypsy women always seem to have a hard look, maybe from living outside around a fire in all kinds of weather. Their wagons were only really used at night to sleep in.

I remember me father when me granny Minty died it was the first time I'd ever seen him cry and it felt like a knife in me heart for I knowd only great pain could bring him to tears. An' yet on the day of the funeral, he didn't shed a tear. My Pearly, me sister an' me held on to him trying to comfort him, but he shook us off in case people would think we was holding him up. Even at his mother's funeral he didn't wanna be seen as weak.

Minty lived until she was eighty-nine and her great aunt Britannia Dixie (née Deakins) lived for more than a century. It may be fair to say that both these women were blessed with long lives, since the average life-expectancy of a Gypsy is approximately forty-eight years old.

Gypsy funerals have changed through the years. Gypsies have always 'set up', meaning staying awake all night with the body of the person who died and their family, but where they would set up in the past for anything from two days to a week, not leaving until six or seven in the mornings, now it is only one or two nights they set up for and they will now leave as early as one or two in the morning.

Always in the past the wagon or trailers the dead person came back in would be

Opposite: Photograph taken at the funeral of one of the Stockins (Smiths), Levy Smith's cousins. Mourners (left to right): Muggy, Amos, Joe, Wally Stockins, Johnny, Rhymer

Top: Unrania Boswell (on crutches) at the funeral of her husband, Levi

burnt after the funeral, as would all of their belongings but now because of so many *needies* living in *kenners*, this no longer happens as much. When a Gypsy dies, all the family, cousins, aunts, uncles, nieces, nephews, brothers, sisters, anyone remotely related, will come to the funeral no matter where they are or what they are doing, this is called showing respect, not only for the person that died but for the whole family. Up to a thousand Gypsies can attend a Gypsy funeral, each bringing flowers most times made into something that the person who died liked. The closer related you are to the person who died the bigger and better the flowers you would have made for 'em.

Black is always worn on the day of the funeral out of respect and for close family. Black is worn for a year after the funeral, unless the person who died asked when alive for this not to be.

The Funeral of Levi Boswell *described by Mary Chambers*
Gypsy Levi Boswell was laid to rest at the age of 78. His casket half hidden in flowers

Funeral of Levi Boswell, St Giles' church, Farnborough

was in a hearse drawn by six horses. At the graveside flocked Gypsies from near and far.

The crippled wife of Levi Boswell, Urania, made a pathetic figure, leaning on crutches sported by her five children.

Levi and Urania had five children, three boys and two girls, two of the boys were born crippled and died young. They are buried in the same grave as Levi and Urania in Farnborough, Kent.

Urania Boswell (formerly Lee) was born 1851. Urania's father was Abraham Lee born 28 June 1830 and her mother was Mary Smith.

In the spotlight

Granny Emily Smith *by Lindsey Marsh*

My granny Emily was the youngest of the family born in 1927 and when her mom Eliza was dying she went to live with her mom's (Cooper) family as she was only a baby. Gran grew up in Mitcham mainly as she stayed with her aunts Pashey and Uni, their husbands Barney and Wheeny and her granny Amy.

Every now and then gran went to school, although this wasn't very often so she could read and write, but only very little and she couldn't understand the time. As a young girl gran could make wooden pegs and flowers and she had long fair coloured hair, which turned so dark it was almost black as she got older.

During the war gran fell in love with a *gorger* soldier named Ivor (Ivan) and after the war they married in Morden where they were stopping at and then ran away to Shrewsbury to live with Ivan's family. Gran always missed her family and when she could, she would go back to visit them all, otherwise she would write to her aunt Uni who would also write back.

Gran had five *chavvys* with Ivor and when they later split up, she met my granddad Fred and had five more and two of these were twins, although she lost one as a baby. My mom Jenny is the youngest of them all.

Mom and auntie Sylvie have always enjoyed

Emily Smith (daughter of Derby and Eliza)

telling us stories about gran as she got up to all sorts of stuff and uncle George often has his moments of storytelling too! Auntie Sylvie said that gran used to tell her, her nickname was 'Peach', as she once had pneumonia as a girl and when she came round, the first thing she asked for was a peach.

As told to Lindsey Marsh by Jenny Marsh

Me mom used to say we're going calling today, and take us four kids out raggin (knocking people's door asking for any unwanted clothes). She'd take the pram and me and me brother would sit in it and she'd fill it up with all the stuff people were giving her, so then we'd have to walk with the other two as well. She'd keep some of the clothes to dress us with and then weigh the rest in at Jimmy Rollinsons scrapyard coz they used to give you *luver* for this then. Mom would push the pram all the way from Urban Gardens down to Haybridge and walk everywhere and anywhere. She'd go to different places each week. Mom always knew who the best callers were, who'd call us in and give us something to eat so we could fill our bellies up, while giving mom the rags.

George (brother) and dad would go out killing rabbits and pheasants and that, and then mom would skin them on the doorstep and stick it in the pot to make a good stew for us *chavvys*. Mom would also chop up raw veg like carrots and swede and put it in a saucepan, sprinkle in some oxo cubes and then when it boiled we'd drink it like soup to warm our bellies up.

Mom never liked using electric as she was frightened of it, she wouldn't use an iron, or hoover, she'd use a broom. Mom was spotlessly clean, she used to go mad when I'd hide the rubbish under the carpet coz of wanting to get out playin when I was little! She used to dress us nice as well. If we were lousy she'd sit there crackin' the *jubs* out our hair and we used to say 'can I crack the next one mom'! She'd stand there scrubbing clothes in the sink with her bangles on coz she liked her jewellery and then have us help her put them through the mangle. She'd always teach us how to hang the clothes on the line properly 'so the wind would blow through them'.

Her favorite plants were geraniums and the window sill would be covered in the plants and flowers she'd go *choring* out of peoples gardens. She'd wear a head scarf and keep her fags in her pinny – she'd smoke Senior Service.

She'd always drink carnation milk in her tea and would never have a white egg in the house and she knew the difference between a frog and a toad. She used to call the old half penny pieces *diddlers* and she'd chuck 'em away coz she could never understand 'em and she'd call a ten pence piece, two bob.

Emily Smith with grandson Tony

Mom was a hard worker, always on the go, if we didn't have money for coal for the fire, we'd go to the woods, chop some wood up and load the pram up with it. Her pram was her motor, she'd always fill it up with something. She loved rooking in the tip and we'd dive in and we'd have a good old look.

In the mornings mom would sort the fire out, pull the back of her dress up and warm her arse. Our Sylv would get embarrassed if Paul (her boyfriend) was there and mom would say something like 'what's the matter with you I borned him, he's like me own lad'. Paul used to get her tap dancing as well!

Mom couldn't drive but she brought a blue van and get one of the boys to go driving us about round Ironbridge and different places. She'd love just going for drives. She used to like going down lanes to see what's about and if she spotted something in someone's garden, she'd go and knock on the door to see if it was any *cushty* and to see if she could have it.

She'd never give a damn if anyone upset her or her family though, she'd never hold back no matter how tall, short, small, fat or thin they were. She would only settle for a decent cup of tea and if she was in a café and it was like bulls blood or cold, there would be trouble. The one time when our Sylv was having problems at school, she marched up to the school and told her to get her coat on. Mrs Shakeshaft the teacher told her to sit back down, then mom said 'if your names Mrs Shakeshaft I'll shake the shit out of ya'! We always laugh about that now.

Me brother upset me mom the once as well and mom went to the coal shed and got the axe. Me brother ran off to his bedroom and she chopped a great big hole in his door,

A real character, Emily Smith on one of her birthdays, 10 May 1976

so he buggered off out the bedroom window quick, as he knew she would have done damage if she got to him – she was that fiery when her head went.

She was always good to people, she'd always put people up for the night and give them something to eat, when she got it. She'd always look after her gran kids, she taught our Sylv how to put a nappy on properly and pin the nappy to the vest so that it didn't ride up the back – she cussed the nurse giving her granddaughter cold milk – aint you got a kettle?

Granny Rose Ripley *by Rosie Smith*
Rose Ripley was wife to Sam and mother to fourteen children, including Lily, Joe and Mark. Rose lived a traditional Gypsy way of life and in the following passages her granddaughter Rosie reflects:

I never knew me granny Rose because she died before I was born, but over the years I've heard many *needies* talk of her, and they always talk about her with great respect. I have heard them *rokker* how she helped bring many a Gypsy baby into the world in her days and doctored many who needed it. Lots of baby gals she born, were named after her and I have had lots of old *needie morts dik* to me and say 'I am named after ya granny Rose'.

I've also heard talk about how me granny Rose no matter how little grub she had, she would always share it and I've been told at times when the family were doing well, how she would make big pots of stew and feed half Corks Pitt. All the *chavvys* would *cur* round to her when they see she had the pot on all knowing their bellies would be filled.

Many times me

Rose Ripley with her grandchildren Rosie, one of the many named after her, and Sam

mum has told me stories about her mum and dad. She'd tell me about how her two half sisters (they had a different dad than me mum) were nurses when the war was on and how me granny would take them up food and things to London and at first they was pleased to see her, but as time went on and they found boyfriends, they would get *alaged* when she would turn up with a basket over her arm looking every bit the Gypsy she was, so would hide from her and pretend not to be there. In the end me mum said she give up going cus it hurt her too much and she would always come home heartbroken. My aunts married *gorger mushes* and the family never really saw them again. Me mum heard that one married an American solder (soldier) and went to live with him in America.

 Me mum also told me about when me granny died; she said her and me dad had been going up the hospital to see her mostly every night, then one night they had a night home with the *chavvys* but me mum got a feeling come over her telling her that she should go to the hospital but she put it to the back of her mind and went to bed. She told me she awoke in the middle of the night and had a feeling that made her and when she did, me granny stood there looking just like she always did and me mum knew me granny was dead. Later when she saw me aunt Kate, me aunt Kate told me mum me granny Rose had asked for her before she died. I have heard many old Gypsies *rokker* stories of ghosts they have seen and know many of the stories are just tall stories but me mum is as honest as they come and would never make a story up let alone one like that about someone she loved. So I know for hundred per cent that it was true and me

Sam and Rose Ripley, 1960s

granny came to her to say goodbye.

Although as I just said many of the ghost stories the old *needies* told was only made-up around the *yog* for entertainment, I still believe many were also true, for in the 'out of way' places they lived and the hours they would be out and about, it's no wonder they would see whatever ghost there was to be seen. I think a lot of old gypsies were gifted in that way to.

Me granddad Sam Ripley was a soldier in the 1914 war, he never talked about his time as a soldier but he was always known to be a brave man, as were his sons and grandsons.

I am named after me granny Rose and I feel proud to have the name of such a good women and loving mother, and grandmother to those grandchildren lucky enough to have known her.

Levy Smith (A father to be proud of) *by Rosie Smith*
Levy me dad has been a father for all of his four children to look up to and although he's not a big man he has always given all of us a big lot of love. From a child I always remember me dad working hard to feed us, over the years I have known him to be a scrapper, roofer, tree topper, dump runner and tarmacer. I've also known him to go out with a grinding barra sharpening knives, pick every fruit you can say and make holly wreaths, he has sold Christmas trees and bric

Above: Levy Smith

Right: Levy Smith aged 12.

a brac at boot sales and to be honest they ain't much he ain't done or can't do with his hands. Not so much now because he is 72, but when he was younger I remember him under his truck, doing just as good as a mechanic could. I have known him to take out blown up engines and put new ones in all within a day, with me mum bringing him a cup of tea at least every hour and making sure he had *sank* to eat cuz me dad was always one when he was working to forget to eat, but me mum (like the caring person she is) was always there to make sure he did have grub.

Me mum and dad I feel truly have a love story, for they both love each other as much today as they did all them years ago when they first met. Me dad has always told us (his *chavvys*) that from the first time he started courting me mum he known she was the only one for him. Over the years me mum and dad ain't always had it easy; when they first took off when me mum was 17 and me dad was 23 all they had was each other and their love but that was enough for them and together they worked doing the best they could until they earned enough to get their first trailer and from then on they went from strength to strength. Don't get me wrong, me dad has never been a rich man but he has always had a nice home, decent motor and plenty of grub to eat and for me dad that was always enough. Because me dad has never been one to worry about money or

Brothers Levy, Aaron and Jasper Smith with friends

Lily and Levy Smith with a wagon made by Levy

material things, the only thing that has ever mattered to him was that the ones he loved was all well and happy and if they were, so was he. I remember as a child whenever one of us *chavvys* was ill how he would worry himself to death over us. I remember when I was thirteen and had me appendix out he almost had a breakdown with worry about me. Him and me mum wouldn't even leave the hospital at night to go home to bed, they laid outside in the motor to be close to me. Things like this was what my dad would always do as he loved us so much. The only fault I could find in me dad, if I had to find one, was that he worries about us too much which sometimes can be a burden. But still I wouldn't change him for the world.

Me dad, by all who know him, is known as a comic for he is at his happiest when he is either acting the clown to make people laugh or telling one of his many funny stories. As *chavvys* at night me and me brothers and sister would lay in bed and listen to him tell stories that would have us straining our ears to listen. My favourite stories me dad would tell, was the ones he told us, that his dad had told him when he was a small boy about Old Bill. Although he would tell us the same stories over and over again we never seem to got sick of hearing them, even though we all knew the words he was going to

Top: Levy Smith acting the clown

Left: Levy Smith

Levy Smith (with the hat on) was about ten when this family photo was taken. Pictured are five of his brothers, two sisters, his mum and aunt Emily and her two chavvys. Right to left: Frank 'Mushy', Aunt Emily, her daughter and son, Uncle Jasper, grandmother Minty, holding Abraham, Rachel, Lou, Levy, Wally and Aaron, 1940s

say before he even said them. Whenever me dad tells a story he seems to put so much meaning in to the words that as a child I felt like Old Bill was a part of our family and even now at the age of 35 I can't help but have a listen when I hear him telling one of the grand *chavvys* a story about Old Bill.

My father has always told us a story his father had heard a Gypsy family had had the children taken away because they were unclean and *jubby* and had got scared that his children would be taken away, so had sent my granny Minty with all the money that they had at the time, to buy new clothes and bedding for the children. He said they were all washed and the boys' heads had been shaved and the girls hair cut very short, their old clothes and bedding had been burnt and the wagon had been scrubbed from top to bottom and my father said that they had stopped on their own for a time, for fear that the children would pick up *jubs* off the other children. It would have been easier for my father's family if some of the eldest children were girls, for then they would have washed and seen to the younger ones when my granny went out with her basket, but it was only the younger ones that were girls so they straggled on best they could, until some of the boys married and the girls got older.

Jasper Smith *by Lindsey Marsh*
Uncle Jasper was always proud of his Gypsy heritage and the fact he became not just a popular Romany recording artist, but a Gypsy activist too is a testament to this.

He campaigned with the Sevenoaks Gypsy Liasison Committee and was a founder member of the Gypsy Council. The Gypsy Council itself was formed 10 December, 1966 in the Bull, in St Mary's Cray where Jasper and a number of others (including Grattan Puxon) attended a meeting to set it up. This venue had been specifically chosen because it had 'No Gipsies' painted by the entrance, a sign which Jasper and his fellow Councillors hoped to make illegal. Jasper hoped that by helping to set up the Council he would be able to help change the way Gypsies were treated and perceived in society, to allow them to live their traditional Gypsy way of life, as Gypsies were constantly facing harassment and being evicted from their stopping places. He wanted Gypsies to have equal access to all things, including education and welfare and as a result he became a well respected Romany leader.

Jasper also campaigned for Gypsy sites in Kent and Surrey and as a result the local authority provided one of the first council Gypsy sites in Edenbridge, which Jasper and his family even stayed in for a while. After Edenbridge, Jasper moved to the site in Cox Lane, Epsom, and when the council threatened to close this, he protested by building a 25ft high 'Rocket to the Moon' display out of cardboard to illustrate how they might as well live in the sky, as the council wouldn't give them anywhere on land to live their Gypsy way of life. This display even caught attention of the local media.

Jasper also mediated between travellers and the local council, helping advise Epsom Council in setting up more Traveller sites and also the Gypsy Projects Manager in Surrey. In 1971 he attended the first World Romani Congress where he was involved in discussions with people from over eight different countries on

Jasper Smith, 1970s

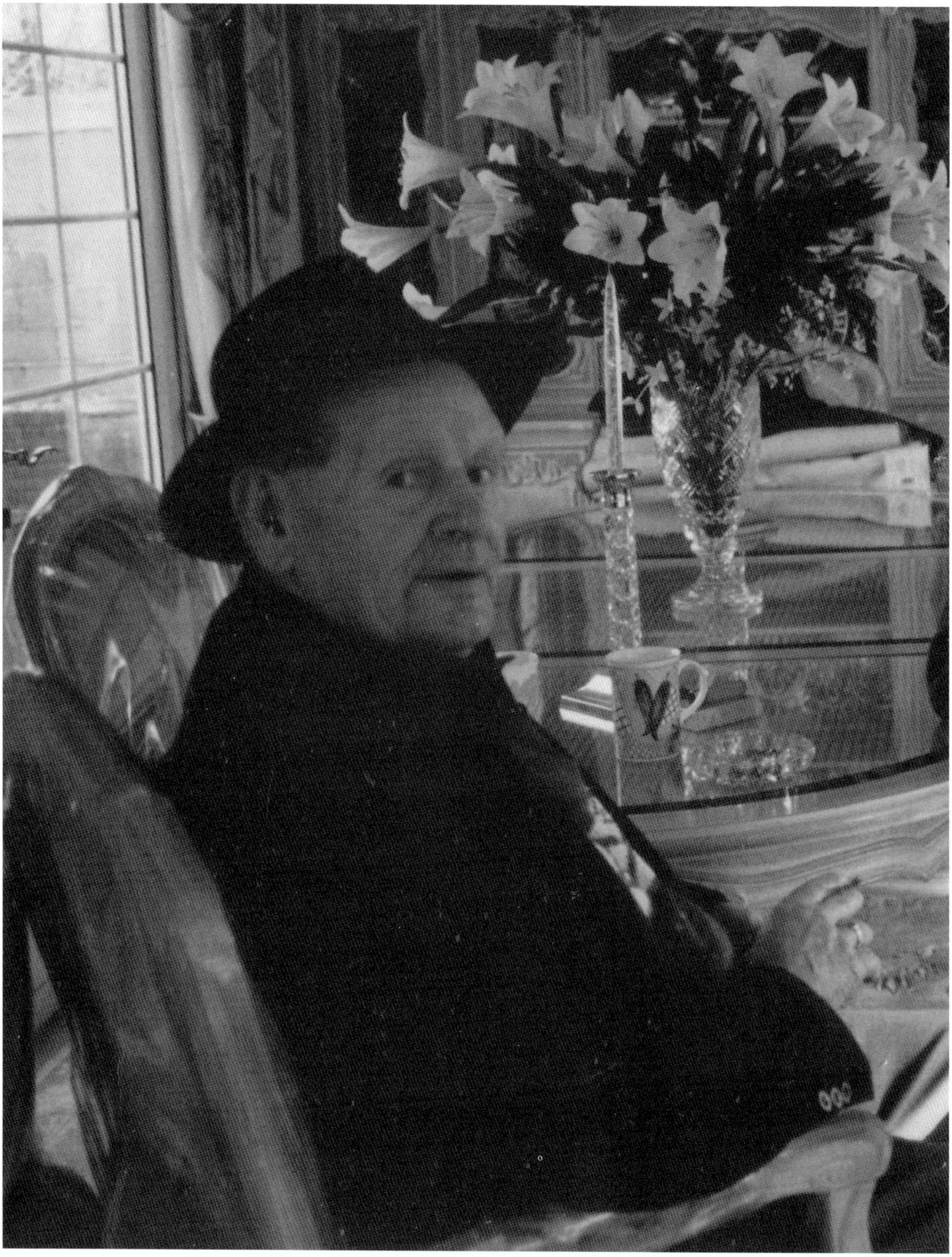

issues relating to language, culture, rights and the wellbeing of Gypsies.

Jasper died 16 April 2003 in hospital, in early hours of the morning. At his funeral there were a hundred vehicles and the traditional 'Chair of Flowers', to symbolize how the Traveller is now resting. An account of his funeral was even published in the local paper *Epsom, Ewell and Banstead Post*, 7 May 2003.

Roma Nation day which also took place near the first anniversary of his death (8 April 2004), was in part a tribute to Jasper and other Travellers including 15-year-old Johnny Delaney who was kicked to death in a racial attack in May 2003.

Opposite: Jasper Smith – a man of great status in the Romany community

Gypsies and discrimination

Jasper Smith with his son, Jasper, washing his plot, Epsom, Surrey

Gypsies and Travellers have been the victims of discrimination for centuries and for some people when they think of the word 'Gypsy', they immediately think of dirty people, littered fields, being cursed, children being stolen and the like. Yet the truth is that Gypsies are only human!

The Gypsies of today deserve nothing but respect as in the past their ancestors survived persecution. In the 1500s for example, a Gypsy could be transported overseas, whipped a hundred times or more, had their ears cut off, sold as slaves and even hanged. Yet even today some people still think it is acceptable to condemn people they don't even know. It's worth remembering that during the second world war 500,000 Gypsies were murdered in Europe.

By Rosie Smith

Gypsies are thought of by most *gorgers* as dirty, unclean people. Many times I have read or heard the words 'dirty Gypo', but in fact most Gypsies are spotlessly clean in their trailers, with many rules on what they would and wouldn't do with regards to cleanliness, such as we would never wash our hands and face in the same bowl or sink that we washed our crockery and pots in and a Gypsy women seen using the same bowl or sink would be seen as *slumicky* and not took tea or food from by other Gypsy families. Also most Gypsies would not have their pets inside their trailers as this is also seen as dirty. Pets, although loved, would be kept outside most times, running free around the *atchin tan*.

Gypsies today are still labelled as being work-shy and for 'sponging off the system', yet it's a well known fact that many Gypsies (including children and grandparents) have worked on the land for centuries and many even fought in the army in two world wars.

Jasper Smith, for example, was just one of the many brave soldiers who risked his life to protect and serve a country that persecuted his ancestors. Men like Jasper deserve huge respect. Thanks to people like him we can enjoy the freedoms we have today.

Jasper was a good man, with strong values, yet it seemed that whatever he did, it was never enough, just because he was born Gypsy. Up until the late 1970s for example, pubs such as the Swan and Sugarloaf in Croydon refused to serve Jasper and his family a single drink, because of their Gypsy blood and lifestyle.

By Rosie Smith

One of my earliest memories as a child was when I was about three or four. We had

Rosie Smith aged three with her mum Lily, 1970s

Levy Smith shaving in the chrome of his trailer, 1970s

pulled along the side of the road for the night on our way to wherever we were going at the time and I'd been sleeping in bed in the middle of the night when I was awoke by the sound of bangs; something was hitting the side of our trailer which scared me and I started to cry and I remember my father jumping out of bed and searching for his trousers in the darkness. I could hear men outside shouting swear words as well as 'dirty gypo'. My brothers, who were sixteen and fourteen at the time, were already up and dressed and waiting ready to follow my father outside to face the men, which they did, only to see a car pull away. The next morning I can remember both my mother and father being very upset by the dents in our beautiful trailer. The men had done hundreds of pounds of damage to our trailer, but *gavvers* were never contacted and my dad just moved on to our next stopping place next day like he had planned. But after that night, as a child, the slightest sound in the night would have me terrified.

Gavvers and Government Bodies

The relationship between Gypsies and the police has gradually improved over time, although for many, it could still be better. In the past Gypsies were often bullied by the police as Robert Dawson describes in his book *Crime and Prejudice: Traditional Travellers* (2000), with police officers deliberately kicking burning sticks onto Gypsy children only to see that they move on quickly.

By Rosie Smith

Gypsies had very little rights in them days and the *gavvers* would bully them badly but there was not much they could do about it cuz to stick up to the *gavvers* meant a time served inside. So the families would be moved on all hours, day and night. Most times their only hope of spending some time somewhere was if they would get permission off some kind landowner to stay on his land or they would find a place so far out the way it would be a time before anyone even realised they were there.

Back when me dad was a small boy (maybe six or seven), there was a farmer and old *gavver* who hated Gypsies and made it their life's work to prosecute them. It was the farmer who would go out of his way to find where the Gypsies were stopping, then he would go get the *gavver* and together they would move the family involved on, but not only would the *gavver* move them on, but he would also kick pots of food off the *yog*, much to the distress of the hungry children and rip down the bender tents, or if he came in the middle of the night, come up into the wagon where they were sleeping, shouting and ripping the blankets off them. One time when he came me granddad was sitting around the *yog* and the *gavver* run there and kicked the fire so the fire brands went all over me granddad Frank and burnt him. Me granddad jumped up, even though he was in pain he had it in he's mind to hit the *gavver* so rushed at the *gavver*, but me granny jumped in front of him and so did a couple of the older boys (me dad's brothers), as they were holding him the *gavver* was tormenting me granddad saying "come on gypo hit me, then you will go down for a very long time" to which me granddad shouted back "I'd do life for you, you mothers cunt", me granny was screaming and the *chavvys* was crying, and me granny was begging to me granddad to stop cus he would be took away. I'm not sure if it was me granny's begging or the *chavvys* crying, but me granddad backed down and packed up and they moved on. Me granddad was burnt badly on his chest and suffered a lot of pain because of it, but in them days there was no one to go to for help and Gypsies just had to suffer whatever the *gavvers* dished out if they didn't wanna go to prison, but saying all this there was the odd good *gavver* that would turn a blind eye to them stopping in their district, as long as ya never left no mess or caused any trouble. I'm not sure if it's true, but I heard a story that the same *gavver* raped a young Gypsy girl from another Gypsy family and then went missing and was never seen again. It was rumoured among the Gypsies that the brother of the girl killed him, for you could rip down our tents, burn our chests, kick our pots of stew off the fire and get away with it, but touch our women and that's a different matter.

It gets me so upset when I hear all the bad things Gypsies are meant to do but never is it said what we have had done to us, over the years being bullied by *gavvers*, government council, teachers and just gorgers in general. And although things are getting better, still we get discriminated against in a time and age when people should know better. Recently my daughter was being called "pikey" at school, she told a teacher and the teacher simply said well you are one. My daughter answered, no I'm not a "pikey" or "Gypo", I am a Romany Gypsy traveller. When she came home and told me what had happened, I couldn't help but wonder if she had been black and called "nigger" would it still be ok. Luckily things like this don't happen much anymore, but I feel that it shouldn't happen at all, not by teachers at least.

Norman Dodds – A *Gorger* Who Cared
Norman Dodds was the Labour MP for Erith and Crayford from 1955–65 who fought

for Gypsies. He was one of the few outside the Gypsy community who took time to get to know them. Although Dodds died in 1965, he instigated the campaigns which lead to Parliament passing the Caravans Act in 1968, an Act which required all local authorities in England and Wales, to provide sites which Gypsies could live in their caravans on, either temporarily or permanently.

Dodds actively campaigned for Gypsies and often interacted closely with the Travelling community to best understand their needs. He was a man who Gypsies greatly respected.

By Rosie Smith

Me mum and dad always talk of what a good man MP Norman Dodds was and how he tried his hardest for them when they was being evicted from Dartford Woods. At the time me brother was just three weeks old and the last thing me mum wanted was to be on the road with a three week old baby in winter. When they left Dartford Woods they pulled along the side of the A2 which was a busy dangerous road, it wasn't the place they wanted to be, but at the time they had nowhere else to go. Many nights were me

Right: Norman Dodds MP talking to Rose Ripley and her son George, Dartford Woods

Opposite top: Norman Dodds MP with the Ripley family

Opposite bottom: Funeral of Norman Dodds. Left to right: Levy Smith with son, Nelson Duval, Lily Smith with son, Mark Ripley and Sam Ripley

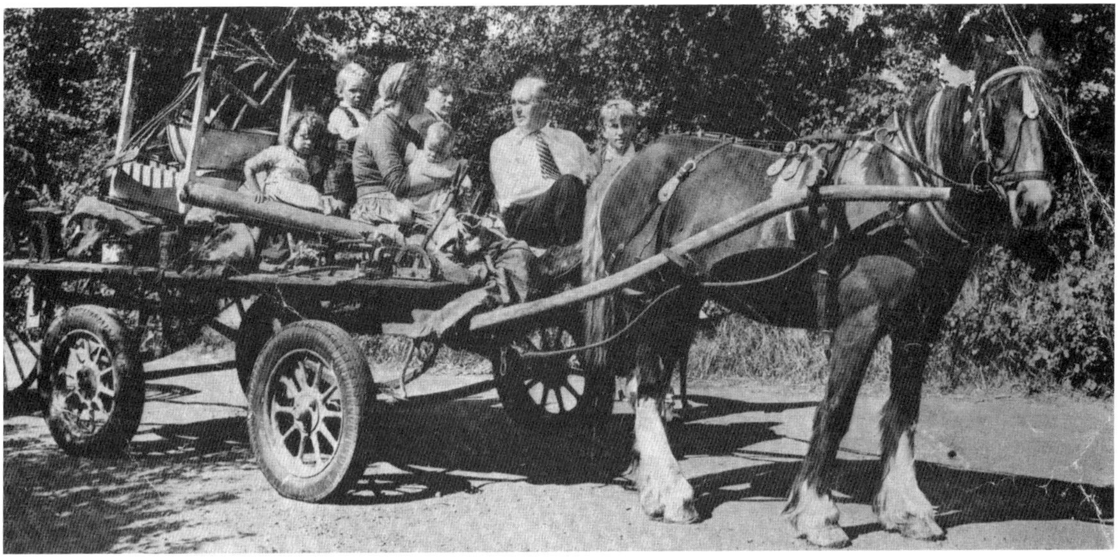

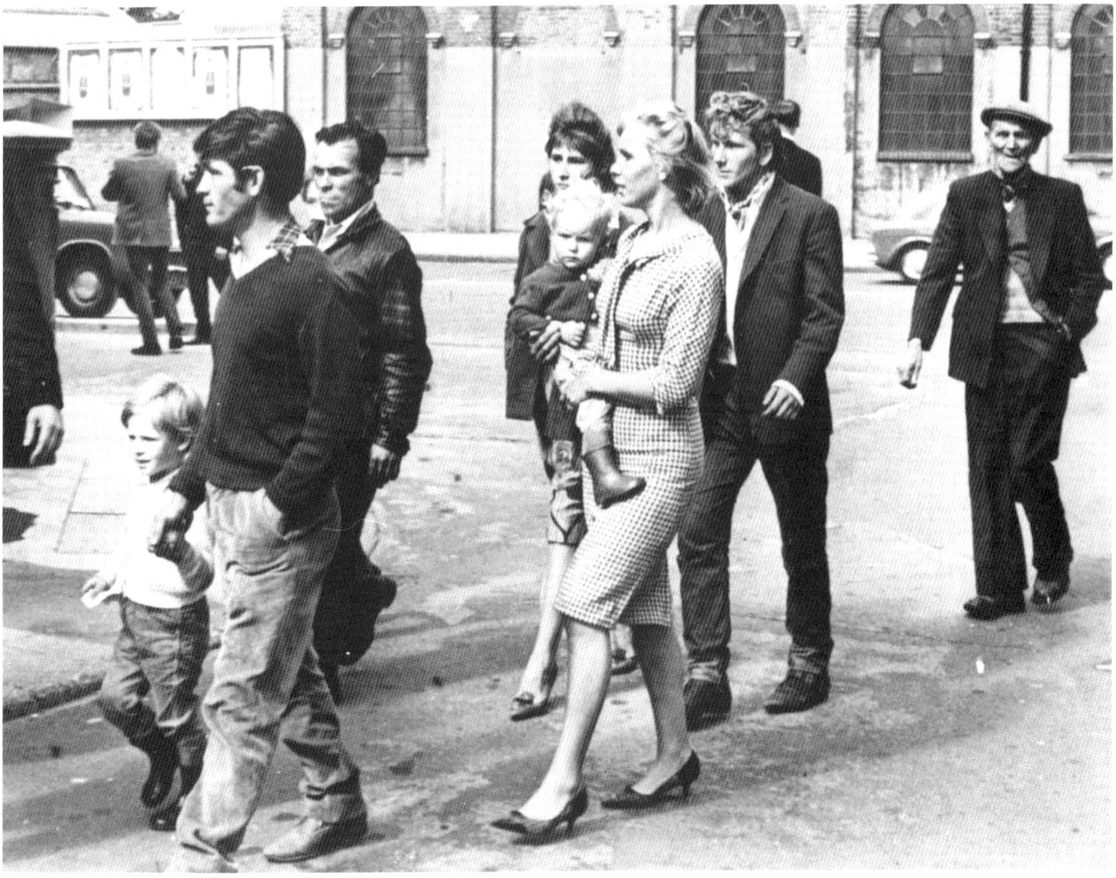

Top: Rose Ripley with local council officers before eviction from Dartford Woods

Bottom: The eviction

Top: Eviction from Dartford Woods

Left: Gypsies stopping along the A2 after they had been evicted from Dartford Woods

mum and dad and other Gypsy families stopping there, pelted with stones, for *nank* else, only cuz they was Gypsies.

Guns, Bombs, Sirens and Smiths

Jasper Smith was born 25 June, 1921 in wagon, in Walton Lane, Epsom, Surrey. Although Jasper was just six years old when his mother died, he went on to lead an eventful life.

As a young adult, Jasper fought in the army during the second world war, when hundreds of thousands of Gypsies were murdered in the gas chambers of the Nazi concentration camps.

Whilst Jasper was away in the army, his family, including his widowed dad, Derby, were all living in a Gypsy *vardo* in Surrey. Jasper's older sisters, Minty and Amy, who had already lived through the first world war (as children aged three and one), were now having to experience it again as adults in their late twenties.

With the men away at war, Jasper and Minty's baby sister Emily was just one of the many women who had to carry on with the men's jobs. Emily worked in the famous munition factory at the Royal Arsenal, in Woolwich, south-east London.

On the day of 7 September 1940, London came under attack in what's known as the London Blitz. London was bombed for hours by hundreds of German war planes in two separate attacks. In order to force the country to surrender, Hitler's plan was to destroy the city, before invading it on land.

By Rosie Smith

Me granny's brother Jasper had all the qualities a gypsy man should have, he was a brave and proud man, who had honour and respect. Many stories me dad (Levy) has told me about him and the more he told me of him, the more I liked him and maybe in a way it's only him I got to thank for being here today for if not for him who knows what would have happened to me dad. In the war me uncle Jasper was a soldier, so did his bit for our country like many other Gypsies, although this is never *rokkered* about by *gorgers* – so many times have I heard how Gypsies do this bad thing or that bad thing, which maybe true because Gypsies is just people like everyone else and there are good ones and bad ones, but it seems to be the bad ones get

Jasper Smith a Gypsy soldier in his teens in the Second World War

rokkered about and yet the good ones like me uncle Jasper get forgotten. Anyway back to me story, me uncle Jasper was home on home-leave and stopping with me granny Minty and granddad Frank. They were all in the bed in the middle of the night, me granny and granddad up inside the wagon with the youngest children and the gals, and me uncle Jasper was laying under the wagon with the older boys, when the sarings (sirens) started to go off, they all jumped up and started to run to the shelter, me granddad and uncle Jasper carrying some of the smaller children and me granny carrying me dad in his blanket. As they were running me granny dropped me dad out of the blanket but was so afraid she just kept running. When she reached the shelter and me uncle Jasper asked her where me dad was, me granny started screaming he was outside. By this time bombs were dropping and they could hear them going off, but me uncle Jasper, without a second thought of his own safety, run out to get me dad and bring him back to the shelter which he did safe and sound, but next morning when they came out of the shelter, right where my dad had lay, a bomb had hit so maybe without my great uncle Jasper me dad would not be here today and neither would I.

The bombing carried on day and night until May time the following year, and so for eight consecutive months, sounds of sirens wailing, guns blasting and bombs exploding, occupied the city. Fires everywhere escalated out of control, schools, cathedrals and more than a million houses were hit, including the Royal Arsenal factory where young Emily worked. Time after time, Minty and her family, would run for the sake of their lives to the underground stations and air raid shelters and at the end of the blitz over forty-thousand civilian lives were claimed.

By Rosie Smith

Another time me uncle Jasper came home on home-leave and when he got to me granny and granddad, he found them in a bad way me granddad was laid up in bed ill and me granny was anytime having one of the *tiknas* so neither one of them could go out and get *nank* so they was all *clamming*. Me uncle Jasper got the old ferret me granddad had on the back of the wagon and went straight off rabbiting, later he came back with five or six rabbits then gutted and cleaned them, then took them off to the old butcher to sale em when he came back he brought back tea, sugar, bread, butter, potatoes and such, and granny made a rabbit stew with one of the rabbits they had keep and they all had a good bellyful thanks to me uncle Jasper. He fed them all like that till he went back off leave by which time me granddad was back on his feet, me dad told me his uncle Jasper would never see any of the family go hungry and many a time feed the family in just this way me dad said. He was always a man for his family and wouldn't even have wind blow on his sisters. Many a time he would get rowing with me granddad Frank other me granny cus me granddad would come home from the pub and start a row with me granny and me granny would scream and shout and then me uncle Jasper would run in and get me granny out nine times out of ten getting rowing with me granddad. They would always say they would fight next morning but when next morning come they would all get up like *nank* ain't happen neither of them holding a grudge. Me dad said he was a good uncle to his brothers and sisters' *chavvys* and if any of the other *needie* men was telling them off he would be the first one to step forward and talk up for them whether they was right or wrong he just wouldn't have anything said to any of his family he would get out to anyone for them no matter who the man was or how good a name he had. Me uncle Jasper would step up to him, he was a brave man and yet he never liked or caused trouble.

Changing Times – Childhood, Education and Language

Gypsy life in Britain has changed radically over time, when you compare the life which those Gypsies who entered England in the 16th century would have experienced, to the life the Gypsies of today lead. Whilst many changes have been positive, in the sense Britain no longer hangs people for being a Gypsy, others have been negative; like caged birds, Gypsies, whose tradition has always been to travel are now forced to settle in houses or in council sites.

By Rosie Smith

One of the things that really hurts me, is knowing my *chavvys* will never know a childhood like I did. Don't get me wrong, I know there was things I missed out on like; a good education, but still I feel I knew a better childhood than ever they will know. As a child my life always seemed to be filled with something new happening, somewhere new to go, or something new to see and someone new to meet, but it seems all my children know is school and telly and computer games. I look at them sometimes when the sun is shining and they is sat watching telly and my heart breaks because I know on a day like this, I would have been out running wild with the other Gypsy *chavvys* we would be stopping with, climbing trees or playing chase or just playing, full stop.

The only thing I am really glad about is that I feel my *chavvys* will never know the bullying or racism I suffered as a child because I feel in this age the world is getting better for Gypsies, for although there is still many racist people out there, in no way is it as bad as it was when I was growing up, when you couldn't even walk into a shop without being watched all-around and school was more like going to be tortured every day, than going to learn, and not only from the other *chavvys* but from the teachers too. How many times I have been called 'Gypo' and 'pikey' I could not count. I know some of the Gypsy *chavvys*, that didn't look or talk as Gypsy as me, would *sham* they weren't even *needies*, because they was so *trashed* of being bullied. Don't get me wrong, most *needie chavvys* is as brave as they come, but when you is in a school full of *gorgers* and you are the only Gypsy, or maybe just one of a couple of Gypsies or more, then it wasn't so easy to be brave. But myself even as a child I was always so proud of what I was and wouldn't have *shammed* to be something else even if I could have got away with it, which I couldn't. Luckily my *chavvys* at school have never even had to think about *shamming* being *sank* they weren't, because they are liked by their *gorger* friends and teachers, and are well liked and settled in school. It made me so proud when at school, when the *chavvys* had to do a project on a topic of their choice, my daughter chose to do it about Gypsy lifestyle, wanting her friends to see what her background was like, for she is just like I was at her age and is proud of what she is, only difference is where I got bullied because of it, she got golden work and student of the week for it!

Left: Levy and Pearly Smith

Below: Stopping in a cherry orchard, Pembury, Kent

GYPSIES AND DISCRIMINATION

It's so sad but the Romany language is also slowly being lost, with teenage Gypsies knowing little or no Romany words. Even Gypsies in their 30s and 40s know less than half of what their parents did before them. Some Gypsies of today, when told very old Gypsy words, laugh, as they don't even believe that the words were ever used.

The Romany language originated in India but has absorbed many European influences, so there are many different dialects. The language reached the UK in the 16th century when the first Romany Gypsies came to England and spoke this fluently and it wasn't until the 19th century that English took over as the everyday language for Gypsies and became more mixed with Romany words.

Our *rokker* is slowly dying out and unless Gypsies pass it down to their *chavvys* in the next 20 or 30 years, it will be gone. Even from when I was little words seem to be lost cuz I know words that are never used now, but I know they must have been used when I was little, cuz how else would I know them? Our language is part of what makes us what we are so we should do more to try and keep it, by teaching what we know to our *chavvys* and re-learning what we have forgotten.

Aaron Smith in a toy 'silky'

Poems

The Road
Gypsy Roselouise

I'm settled on a site the way I'd never thought I'd be,
But always in my heart, the road is calling me.
The memories of my childhood running wild and free,
Are always in my mind causing longing deep in me.

In winter I am happy, to be pulled up on my plot,
For I know in winter to be settled means a lot,
But when I see the sunshine my feet begin to itch,
And I feel imprisoned on this site I long to ditch.

The beauty of the road is not there for all to see,
Some in houses and on sites are happy there to be.
They've forgot about the good old days on the open road,
All they remember is the hunger and the dirty clothes.

But I remember raindrops falling on my trailer roof,
And the cushty trotting sound of the horses hoofs.
In every different town a cousin we would meet,
Sitting round a yog at night, with them you couldn't beat.

In the morning in the summer as the day began,
I'd hear my father playing his accordion.
Now on summer mornings all that I can hear,
Is my chavvys with the telly blurring loudly in my ear.

Fruit picking in the summer we always did in Kent,
In the cherry orchard was the best time that I've spent.
If I could go back in time I know right where I'd be,
Sitting on a cherry box as my father played for me

Ode to a Gypsy Queen
Gypsy Poet RighteousLeviprice

I've been a Gypsy man all of my life, and had my share of problems and strife.
I've worked like a dog, blood, sweat and tears, hard roads, hard old days, hard old years.
Each night before bed I look up to the sky, and sometimes I wonder just how I've got by.
With no education and hated everywhere I go, a million times I've heard the word "no".
I've walked the hard miles, for many a year, I've fought my demons; I've fought my fear.
I've struggled on up life's never ending hill, often I've wondered from where comes my will.
But things aren't always as bad as they seem, my most valuable possession is my Gypsy queen.
Though life is hard, unfair and can be so cruel, my woman is my God, in my crown, the jewel.
We jumped over the broomstick at age seventeen, and for fifty long years my saviour she has been.
Shoulder to shoulder, we've travelled through life, through thick and thin I've relied on my dear wife.
When I have been hungry, she has kept me fed, and when I've been drunk she has put me to bed.
When times have been hard she has knocked on doors, God love her, I've seen her feet covered is sores.
She has been my friend, my confidant, and my lover, she is a cook, a cleaner, a workhorse, and a mother.
I've never laid a hand on her, that wouldn't be fair, besides she can punch like a man, I wouldn't even dare!
She gave me eight children, each one fit and strong, though once again we are two, for the children are gone.
They're all grown up now, and have families of their own, but my wife and I are so close, we work better alone.
Some men dream of money and those men make me sigh, for I know life's secret; some things money can't buy.
Money can't buy you love, nor can it buy you a friend, it can't give back your youth, nor a broken heart mend.
Possessions can be replaced, and as long as you have health, don't neglect life's essentials, don't worry about wealth.
A kind word or a tender touch from the woman you love, can cure all life's ills; and life's stress, make you rise above.
So to my woman, my sweetheart, I will say this to you, without you in my life, I don't

know if I'd have gotten through,
You've made me the man I am, you've defined my whole life: My woman my darling, my very best friend, my precious wife.

Old Gypsy Blood
Gypsy Roselouise

My father's a traveller an old gypsy man, He lives in a trailer he calls his old tan,
He sets around a yog, till late in the night, Story's he'll rokker to its almost day light.
My mother's a traveller with old gypsy blood, her heart filled with gypsy motherly love,
She knows how to cook to scrub and to clean, she will bring a good shine, to any old thing.
They live in a trailer that sparkles and shines, there's china around all different kinds
Crown Darby and Ainslie and lots of cut glass, Collected by my mum in the years that have passed.
They live on a site that's just out of sight; there are woods to the left and fields to the right.
My father as a dog it's an old lurcker juk, they go get a rabbet for my mother to cook.
On Sunday they have rabbet pudding or stew, wash down with tea and one cup won't do.
Mum makes the best tea we all know that it's true, that's why for my father no one else's will do
My father as a lorry it's an old transit truck he takes it to work with his ladders on the back
He looks for a gronta to cut down her trees, if he gets her money then he's eager to please
My father and mother are two of the best, their love for us chavvy's we don't have to test
That's why their chavvy's all live around because no better place could we ever have found

Picture gallery

Lindsey Marsh with Dan and children Shannon and Danny

Rosie Smith, aged 18, with Rosie Baker

OLD WAYS, NEW DAYS

90

*Right: Pearly
Smith (Rosie
Smith's daughter)
inside their chalet*

*Opposite: Levy
Smith (Rosie
Smith's brother)*

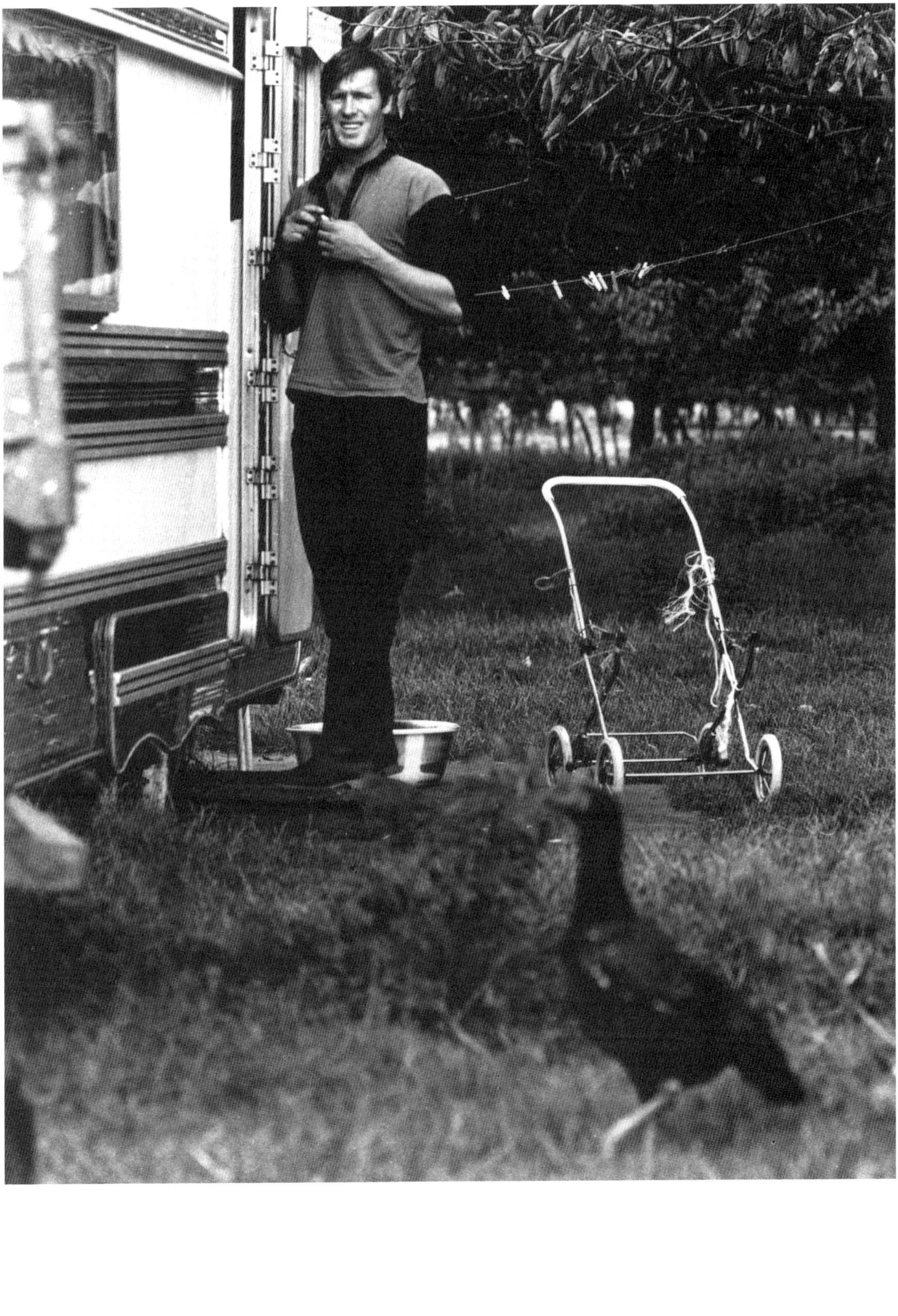

Above: Stopping in Kent

Right: Jasper Smith (right) with his son and grandchildren, Cox Lane, Epsom

PICTURE GALLERY

*Gypsy children,
Star Lane site,
Kent, 1970s*

Rachel Smith and family, Kent, 1962

Further sources

The Smith, Cooper and Ripley family has appeared in many sources available to buy. Below is a general reference guide to these:

Books and Journals
Folksongs of Britain and Ireland by Peter Kennedy, Allisson Whyte, Raymond Parfrey

Gypsy Lore Society by Gypsy Lore Society (1999 and 1946)

Gypsy Politics and Social Change by Thomas Alan Acton

Historical Dictionary of the Gypsies (Romanies) by Donald Kenrick

King of the Gypsies by Bartley Gorman

Now Shoon the Romano Gillie by Tim Coughlan

On the Cobbles by Jimmy Stockins

Scholarship and the Gypsy Struggle by Donald Kenrick, Thomas Alan Acton

Stopping Places by Simon Evans

The Folk Handbook by David Atkinson, John Morrish, Vic Gammon, Rikky Rooksby, Mark Brend, Martin Carthy, Nigel Williamson

The Journal of American Folk-lore by American Folklore Society, JSTOR (Organization), Project Muse

Times to Remember by Barrie Law

DVDs and Videos
Travellers Tales by Jake Bowers

Where do we go from here? By Barrie Law

Radio Shows
Rocker Radio (broadcast Sundays 7–9pm on BBC Radio Suffolk)

Television Programmes
Hopping Down in Kent by ITV

Schools Programme by Thames TV

BBC's Folkweave Programme with Ewan McColl

Music CDs
A Story I'm Just About to Tell

Here's Luck to a Man

My Father's the King of the Gypsies (Voice of the People Vol. 11)

Sweet Gypsy Singer Sherrymarie

The Rough Guide to Music of the Gypsies

The Traveling Songster An Anthology of Gypsy Singers

To Catch a Fine Buck Was My Delight

Acknowledgements

Thank you to all who contributed towards making this book and in particular: Gypsy Poet – RighteousLeviPrice, Jenny Marsh, Levy Smith, Lily Smith (Ripley), Mary Chambers, Robert Dawson, author of *Crime and Prejudice: Traditional Travellers* and to Milo Books Ltd, Preston, publishers of *King of the Gypsies* and the *Coventry Evening Telegraph* for permission to use the photograph of Bartley Gorman.

'Fair Play' Smith, Bill Smith, Alf Smith, Alice Smith and Louie Smith, Surrey, 1930s